Praise for HeatherAsh Amar

'HeatherAsh Amara's *Warrior Goddess Training* is a book for the upcoming generation, an antidote to the pervasive pressures of the advertising industry and the public media as to what a woman should be. She has synthesized the teachings of feminism and female shamanism, encouraging modern girls and women to hold their own and claim their authority in a culture that would otherwise objectify and trivialize them.'

– **Vicki Noble**, healer, artist, teacher and author of
Shakti Woman and *The Double Goddess*

'Sisters, it's time to shed the "shoulds", see ourselves through our own eyes instead of others', and close the gap between wishing for and realizing once and for all who we came here to be. No one shows you how to walk this journey with courage and compassionate self-acceptance better than gifted teacher HeatherAsh Amara.'

– **Stephanie Bennett Vogt**, author of *Your Spacious Self*

'HeatherAsh Amara is your coach and impeccable teacher in the life-ceremony offered in this book.'

– **Ana Forrest**, bestselling author of *Fierce Medicine*
and founder of Forrest Yoga

'This is a book for all women, no matter their age or stage of life. HeatherAsh Amara is a master teacher who embodies the concepts of warrior and goddess in her life and writing . . . Each lesson she presents offers insight and practices for spiritual, physical, intellectual and psychological growth.'

– **Judith Yost**, Dean of Students, Wisdom School of Graduate
Studies and author of *Nature and Intimacy*

'In *Warrior Goddess Training*, HeatherAsh Amara shares her experience as a teacher, friend and guide, helping a new generation of women enter their own journey of inner transformation.'

– don Miguel Ruiz, author of *The Four Agreements*

'I am a man. This book wasn't written for me, but I am so glad that HeatherAsh Amara has invited women everywhere to step into their most powerful, natural selves in this way.

Frankly, it is a confusing time for men. Our traditional roles and expectations are changing in major ways, and we need women to meet us with honesty, love and a commitment to themselves. When they do, it helps us make the transition to a more balanced way of relating. Evolving men need warrior goddess women now more than ever.

That is exactly what HeatherAsh Amara is teaching in this wonderful book of hers. I have learned a lot from her in live classes. She has led me on fire walks more than once. She embodies the raw, vulnerable, loving life, and now she is asking other warrior goddesses in waiting to step off the sidelines and join her.'

– Jacob Nordby, founder of Blessed Are the Weird People and author of *The Divine Arsonist*

WARRIOR GODDESS TRAINING

COMPANION
WORKBOOK

WARRIOR
GODDESS
TRAINING

COMPANION
WORKBOOK

HEATHERASH AMARA

HAY HOUSE

Carlsbad, California • New York City • London • Sydney
Johannesburg • Vancouver • Hong Kong • New Delhi

First published and distributed in the United States of America by:
Hierophant Publishing, 8301 Broadway, Suite 219, San Antonio, TX 78209
www.hierophantpublishing.com

Published and distributed in the United Kingdom by:
Hay House UK Ltd, Astley House, 33 Notting Hill Gate, London W11 3JQ
Tel: +44 (0)20 3675 2450; Fax: +44 (0)20 3675 2451; www.hayhouse.co.uk

Published and distributed in Australia by:
Hay House Australia Ltd, 18/36 Ralph St, Alexandria NSW 2015
Tel: (61) 2 9669 4299; Fax: (61) 2 9669 4144; www.hayhouse.com.au

Published and distributed in the Republic of South Africa by:
Hay House SA (Pty) Ltd, PO Box 990, Witkoppen 2068
info@hayhouse.co.za; www.hayhouse.co.za

Published and distributed in India by:
Hay House Publishers India, Muskaan Complex, Plot No.3, B-2,
Vasant Kunj, New Delhi 110 070
Tel: (91) 11 4176 1620; Fax: (91) 11 4176 1630; www.hayhouse.co.in

Distributed in Canada by:
Raincoast Books, 2440 Viking Way, Richmond, B.C. V6V 1N2
Tel: (1) 604 448 7100; Fax: (1) 604 270 7161; www.raincoast.com

Cover design by Emma Smith; Cover art by Elena Ray | Shutterstock; Interior
design by Jane Hagaman; Illustrations by Kevin Flores

A catalogue record for this book is available from the British Library.

ISBN: 978-1-78180-791-0

Printed and bound in Great Britain by TJ International Ltd, Padstow, Cornwall.

Contents

Introduction

Hello Warrior Goddesses! Welcome to the *Warrior Goddess Training Companion Workbook*.

As the name implies, this companion guide is meant to be read either simultaneously with or after you have read the primary book, *Warrior Goddess Training: Become the Woman You Are Meant to Be*.

I know we have some nonconformists in the crowd—I love that about you—and as a result, some may choose to read this companion workbook without reading *Warrior Goddess Training*. That's fine too, but please know that I don't recommend this, as many of the exercises here will make far more sense after you've read the full lessons in the main book.

Now that the disclaimer portion is out of the way, let's jump right in!

As I wrote in *Warrior Goddess Training*, transformation requires action. Not action from the place of "I have to force myself to do this because I am flawed," but healing action from the place of "I love and honor myself for who I am, and I have a desire to go deeper, to stretch, to experiment. I'm ready!"

Transformation takes willingness to step outside our comfort zones, to try new things, and to learn more about ourselves in the process, adjusting as we go along.

To move from understanding to embodiment means getting out of the safety of our thinking and stepping into the messiness of the unknown.

I don't know about you, but I don't like not doing things perfectly the first time. I want to succeed immediately, to nail it on the first try, to be graceful and calm and collected at all times. I don't relish being scared, or frustrated, or unsure of myself. But I have learned to embrace when I am faced with the unknown, when I feel out of my depth, when I am feeling queasy because I'm doing something that terrifies or confuses me. Because I know that the moments of free fall are what will help me find my wings.

The way to master something is to be willing to make mistakes, sometimes spectacular mistakes; to be klutzy, awkward, and, most importantly, to *try again*. And again. And again.

This *Warrior Goddess Companion Workbook* is meant to be just that: a companion with you on each step of your journey to become the woman you are meant to be. Let it be a beacon that illuminates the hidden places within you, that shines bright like the sun on any old fears and unhealthy patterns, and helps you burn away your limitations and struggles. Use this companion as a partner and friend in three Warrior Goddess steps:

Step 1: Commit

Make this companion book yours. Claim your path of healing with all your heart.

Write your name on the inside cover, along with the statement, "I say YES to myself!" Underneath your name and Yes

Statement, draw an image or symbol that represents your Warrior Goddess self.

For those of you who don't like to write in books, this will be your first small step in moving outside your comfort zone. This is a companion book, which means it is a place to hold ink, tears, creased pages, and doodles. Since I can't come to your house and physically hold your hand and cheerlead you through your inner makeover (and bring endless cups of tea and tissues), this book will stand in as your Warrior Goddess confidant, loving butt-kicker, and guide.

Treat this book as a combination coach and journal. Keep it in a safe place so that you are not editing yourself for fear that someone will read your words. Consult it when you are confused or stuck. You don't have to be a "good girl" and start from the beginning and do each exercise before you can go to the next. Be a "bad girl." Write on the pages. Start at the end. Skip things. Do one exercise over and over again. The most important thing is to make it yours and take little bitty steps or grand leaps!

I also encourage you to get a blank notebook just for the purpose of writing down what you find out about yourself on this journey. Many of the exercises require writing space beyond what is included here.

Step 2: Make Space

Set aside time on your calendar to do these lessons, and, if possible, keep this companion book close to you for spontaneous interaction.

Remember, it's easy to say, "I'll get to it"; but we rarely get to things unless we create space for them. So make dates with yourself to do the Warrior Goddess exercises. Bring the book with you to lunch, wake up early and do a page, or if you have to, balance the book on your knee during your kids' soccer/basketball/track/music practices. Invite a circle of friends to join you.

In her book *The Artist's Way*, Julia Cameron invited her readers to make "art dates" with themselves by picking a couple hours a week to do outings to nourish their artist self. I invite you to do the same by making Warrior Goddess dates with yourself. Put a weekly date on the calendar. Go to a café, a park, a museum, or your bathroom. Open to a page. Experiment. Explore. Repeat regularly. Build your Warrior Goddess muscles with repetition.

Step 3: Enjoy

This is an important one: HAVE FUN!

You are going to be asked to stretch, to challenge yourself, to go into the unknown. This companion book is not designed to make you feel safe and comfortable; it is designed to shake up the familiar so you can shed old limitations and step into the boundlessness that you are. Sometimes it will be uncomfortable. Sometimes it will be difficult. Sometimes it will be scary.

Good!

If you have any of these reactions, it means the work is working you.

And instead of worrying about it, I want you to smile.

Remember that each exercise is designed to bring more clarity, spaciousness, and freedom, and to unleash your Warrior Goddess wisdom. Enjoy the journey. Let go of the idea that you need to fix yourself. You are not broken; you are strong, resilient, and powerful.

For those of you in big transitions or challenges, know this: You are not a victim of life unless you decide you are. Your life may be incredibly difficult right now. You may feel victimized by your ex, your kids, your health, or even your community. But no matter the circumstances, you can honor your fear while simultaneously nourishing your power. I'm not asking you to pretend you are not overwhelmed, depressed, or afraid. I'm asking you to keep reminding yourself that you will get through whatever life is presenting you (as many courageous women like you in similar situations have) and be bolder, more resilient, and wiser on the other side.

I've designed this workbook to support you in doing each of the Warrior Goddess exercises at your own pace. You can do one a month, one a week, or whenever the mood strikes. Just as there is no one way to be a Warrior Goddess, there is also no one way to do the *Warrior Goddess Companion Workbook*. At the same time, remember that you will get out of it what you put in. Stay steady in applying the lessons to your life, and you'll find that each day becomes brighter and more joyful—and that when tough times hit, you'll discover a new resilience and inner power.

In the following chapters, I review and expand on the teachings and exercises from *Warrior Goddess Training*, and I have included many new exercises not found in the original book. So whether you've already done every single exercise in *Warrior Goddess Training*, or none of them, or somewhere in between, this companion book will guide you, step-by-step, deeper into your own healing and help you build your self-esteem, rev up your inner power, and take new, authentic actions in the world.

At the end of the book, I have included some of the most common questions and answers from Warrior Goddesses around the world, taken from my online Warrior Goddess Bootcamp and training programs, in-person workshops, and numerous emails

I have received from all of you. I hope these stories and tips will help you as you navigate your own way down the Warrior Goddess path. I love to hear your stories, successes, and experiences, so please contact me once you've had a chance to dive into this companion workbook. Go to www.warriorgoddess.com, and know that I am supporting you from afar as you use the tools in this book to become more authentic, loving, and present in your daily life.

Lesson 1

Commit to You

From
Warrior Goddess Training

Most women know all about commitment. We commit to hiding or exaggerating our flaws, trying to make others happy or comfortable at the expense of our happiness and comfort, supporting other people's dreams at the expense of our own dreams, and/or criticizing ourselves (and others) at every turn. We commit to who we think we should be rather than committing to meeting ourselves where we are. We commit to seeing ourselves through other people's eyes, gauging our self-worth based on their acceptance, rather than witnessing our unique inner beauty and strength. We commit to being nice rather than being real, or we commit to being right rather than being vulnerable . . .

In Warrior Goddess lesson number one, Commit to You, we begin to close the gap between self-rejection and true acceptance; thinking and being; wishing and becoming.

Your commitment to this idea is the activation of your Warrior Goddess power. When your words, thoughts, and actions foster self-abuse and self-judgment, you are using your immense power against yourself.

Committing to your true, authentic, Warrior Goddess self is the beginning of a lifelong journey of living in authenticity.

You are precious, and you are enough. *Exactly as you are.* But, like most women, you likely carry old seeds of fear about not being good enough, smart enough, pretty enough, small enough, or big enough. When these not-good-enough seeds get watered by your own self-judgment and self-limiting behaviors and by the actions of others, they grow into thorny weeds that block out the sun of truth: There is nothing you need to do to be acceptable and loveable; you already are acceptable and loveable.

The *idea* of accepting and loving yourself 100 percent is much easier than the practice of actually doing it. These old ideas of not being enough are deeply ingrained. Remember, committing to yourself is a layered process, and the purpose of it is to say yes to *all of you*—the parts you love and the parts you don't.

The magic happens when you let go of who you wish you were, because in doing so you free up that wasted energy and begin to reclaim your true power. This surrendering of *what is not* allows you to be radiantly, magnetically, and creatively who you really are.

The following exercises are designed to help you do just that.

As with all the exercises in this book, there is no one way to do them. Take the time to complete all three exercises, or pick one, complete it, and then move to another lesson. (You don't have to go in order!) Make this workbook work for you.

Exercises

1.1 Mirror Gazing

I first introduced this practice during a Warrior Goddess Bootcamp. Some women said that it was one of the hardest things they had ever done, but also one of the most rewarding.

We look in the mirror every day, but few of us actually see ourselves. Instead, we see who we are not, the woman we think we are supposed to be, and we are immediately drawn to the areas where we feel we've fallen short. Consciously looking in the mirror is an act of seeing yourself from your heart instead of through the smoky layers of your own idealization and judgment about who you think you should be. Today, let go of the many ideas you have adopted over the years about what constitutes "beautiful," and just look at the beautiful being who is before you. Practice your seeing without story. Also witness what the stories are. Are they true, or are they social constructs? In many cases, these stories need to be rewritten!

For example, when I did this practice, I noticed that I was judging my forehead. I'd never even thought about my forehead until I was in a photo shoot a few years back and someone kept saying, "relax your forehead!" And then I started noticing all the pictures of women with super smooth foreheads, and all the ads about using Botox to get rid of those "unsightly" forehead lines. Soon I became hyperaware of the deep creases in my forehead. Where before they were part of my character, they suddenly became a flaw.

Luckily, I caught myself pretty quickly and was able to stop and just look in the mirror. Yes, I have lines on my forehead. But who decided it was not okay to have lines? Who decided they were "unsightly"? Not me. That is truly a random decision on some invisible fashion person's part! It is the same as someone deciding that having dark skin is good or bad depending on the context.

To change my inner criticism, I started saying what I saw: "I have lines on my forehead." Then I let go of whether this observation was good or bad. I listened to the stories I was telling myself: "I shouldn't have lines, lines are wrinkles, and wrinkles are bad. I really should do something about my forehead wrinkles . . ." (Isn't it interesting how the word "wrinkles" has a negative implication in this context?)

Once I witnessed the negative voices, I could make new choices in how I wanted to relate to my particular unique brand of forehead. I started looking at my whole face instead of zooming in on the one area that I had mistakenly set up to fail by comparing it to pictures of twenty-five-year-old women with creaseless brows. I also set out to appreciate forehead lines of the women I interacted with. Now, when I look into the mirror and see my face, exactly the way it is, I smile. I am committed to being with me, and my forehead, rather than with a fantasy.

Gaze in the mirror for a few minutes every day, noticing the dialogue of your inner judge, while doing your best to not believe it. Instead, let it dissolve in the light of your unique perfection. Take in the full image of your self as it is reflected back to you. Your precious face is a testimony to all of your experiences and all of your wisdom. Look into your own eyes and commit to accepting the gifts, wisdom, and experiences of the one staring back at you.

Do this practice for ten days, noticing your judgments and exploring their fallacy. The first five days of gazing at yourself in the mirror may be rough, as this is when the judge often speaks the loudest, but it will get easier as you keep at it, and the gift of loving yourself exactly as you are is the reward.

In the space below or in your notebook, write about what arises within you or what you notice about yourself as you do this exercise. What features do you judge on the first few days of doing this practice? Can you love those features for being a part of you?

_____

_____

_____

_____

_____

_____

_____

_____

1.2 The Definition of True Power

Lesson

1

From *Warrior Goddess Training*:

> When you watch television or read magazines, what is most reflected in pictures and words is this: Power is defined by how you look, how much money you make, who you are dating/married to, and how you are progressing on your career track.

> From a framework of fear and scarcity, powerful people are the ones who have, in one way or another, acquired

the most sought after or "best" external resources available, be that money, fame, or beauty.

Many of us have spent years tied to this old model of power, where we rate our worth on how we are perceived or what we have attained . . .

From a Warrior Goddess point of view, power is defined very differently. Power is not sought after from the outside, but rather is patiently cultivated from within. Power has nothing to do with money, or fame, or outside appearances, but with our connection to self, love, authenticity, and the inner mystery of life. From the perspective of true abundance and immanent spiritual connection, powerful people are the ones who have the strongest connection to their internal resources.

Our challenge, then, is to be honest with the places we are still pursuing the old modes of power, and move ourselves toward attuning with a new power: our own. This will not be done all at once, but over time as we unhook ourselves from old patterns and agreements, consciously reconnecting to our authentic center."

The following exercise is a modified version of one that appears in *Warrior Goddess Training*, with lines so you can write down the answers. Even if you have done the original exercise, do it again here to learn what has shifted, paying particular attention to the new questions.

What does true power mean to you? (Try to write down your thoughts without internal editing. I encourage you to keep your hand moving!)

True power is:

_____

_____

_____

_____

_____

_____ .

Next, write down, without judgment, where you give your true power away, exchanging it for the old ideas of power. Be careful, the goal here is not more self-judgment. Instead, simply notice where and when you fall into the old behaviors. In so doing, you have an opportunity to choose again the next time the situation arises.

_____

_____

_____

_____

_____

Lesson

1

1.3 Move from Old to New

Please write your answers in the space provided or in your notebook.

1. Where are you still hooked to old reflections of power? When have you put too much energy into showing others and yourself how much money you have, who you

know, or what your job or other external activities are? In what ways have you showed off or played the "big shot"? (Name-dropping is an easy example.) This doesn't mean you can't and shouldn't celebrate your successes, but when you do so with the energy of being the "big shot," you don't honor yourself or those around you; instead you are hooked to the old ideas of power.

_____

_____

_____

_____

_____

2. How are your judgments and fears tied to an old power matrix? When have you compared yourself to others? For instance, in what recurring situations do you beat yourself up by thinking you don't "have enough," or aren't "pretty enough" or "good enough?" Do you ever catch yourself thinking you should be more like someone else?

_____

_____

_____

_____

_____

3. One great way to purge yourself of old ways of power is to name them without making yourself or others wrong. Here are some other questions to help you explore this idea further:

   - Do you find your worth is based on how you look, or is your worth an inner spring based on self-acceptance and respect?

   - Do you base your value on how well you are taking care of everyone else at the expense of yourself, or do you honor the importance of self-care and loving boundaries?

   - Does your strength come from how much money you have, how sexy you are, or who you know, or does it flow from your inner peace and resilience?

_____

_____

_____

_____

_____

_____

Remember, there is nothing wrong with celebrating your beauty, your ability to care for others, or your career achievements; but when you confuse those external things with who you really are on the inside, you become a slave to these transient things.

1.4 Name Your Female Role Models

Who are your female role models? Who do you strive to be like? Why do you admire these particular women? Our role models can be teachers, family members, characters in movies or on TV, public women or private women. Role models and mentors are important because they inspire us and give us courage to take risks.

List three female role models and their Warrior Goddess qualities and actions that inspire you, such as presence, courage, passion, honesty, compassion, or clarity.

Female Role Model	What I LOVE About Her:

Honor the women who inspire you for their contributions and wisdom, but recognize that you are not going to be just like them; do not use them against yourself. Be aware of the sneakiness of self-judgment. Remember, you can't be your mentors exactly because the world needs you to be YOU!

Surrender to your own unfolding, in your own time. Let go of using other women's accomplishments and grace to beat yourself up; instead, find inspiration and motivation in the beauty and skill around you. As you name the women who inspire you, write down what Warrior Goddess qualities and actions they embody, such as presence, courage, passion, honesty, compassion, or clarity.

1.5 Discover New Role Models

The world is full of so many fabulous Warrior Goddess women, and they can be a special inspiration to help us move outside our familiar notions of what's possible in life.

I recently discovered a new heroine: Amanda Palmer. As I read her book, *The Art of Asking*, I found myself falling in love with her crazy wonderfulness and inspired by her expansive creativity. But soon I noticed my inner dialogue was slipping from "Yay, Amanda is a fabulous role model!" to "Too bad you are not like Amanda . . ." I had to grab the reins of that runaway horse away from the desert of comparison and turn it back toward the cool waters of inspiration.

Remember your task as you think about your role models: Keep all your thought-horses turned toward the flowing streams of possibility rather than the parched lands of not-enough. Let's use each other as joyful motivation.

For this exercise, I want you to go to the library or do a Google search and find at least three awesome women you didn't know about. If you feel so moved, please share them on our Warrior Goddess Training Facebook page.

Here are a few names to get you started. Enjoy your exploration!

- Irena Sendler
- Phillis Wheatley
- Elizabeth Blackwell
- Marie Curie
- Rosabeth Moss Kanter
- Sheryl Sandberg
- Prerna Gupta
- Amanda Palmer
- Nikita Mitchell

Additional Gifts

- Committing to yourself is not a one-time event, but something you do over and over again. When you find yourself falling into old behaviors and making commitments that don't nurture who you really are on the inside, simply take note, love yourself, and choose again.

- You have all the power and all the answers you will ever need inside your beautiful self; sometimes you just need a helpful guide to find them. These ten lessons and your supportive sisters who have gone before you can be such a guide.

- Committing to you, finding out who you really are and what you really want, is the most loving thing you can do for yourself and everyone you know. There is no greater gift to the world than living with authenticity.

- Every moment, ask yourself: What am I committing to now? Is this where I want to spend my precious energy? For each yes, celebrate. For each no, adjust accordingly.

Commit
to
You

Lesson 2

Align with Life

From

Warrior Goddess Training

When we align with life, we choose to align with all of life—not just the parts we like or are comfortable with, and not just when everything goes our way. Aligning with life means truly knowing and accepting that aging, death, sickness, natural disasters, accidents, humans and their wacky ways—all these things are bound to alter our course. Aligning with life means understanding that you cannot control the cycles of nature.

The truth is simple: Life is perfectly imperfect, unpredictable, and unexplainable. A Warrior Goddess does not try to control life or even understand it. Our job is to consciously choose what we are aligning with and then let go, and dance in joy and gratitude for every moment of existence.

Lesson
2

Ah, *aligning with life*. So much easier to think about than to do!

When it comes to aligning with life, many of us have an unspoken bargain in place with the Universe: I'll align with life if I like it, if it doesn't hurt, and if I get my way. I'll align with life as long as I can keep my old, safe habits and I don't have to change.

Of course, aligning with life is easy when things are going our way, and super hard when things are not to our liking. But this is our Warrior Goddess task: to align with everything. It doesn't mean we have to like what is happening, nor does it mean that we become doormats and allow people to walk over us. If circumstances can be changed, then we take the action to change them! But the challenge comes when we are met by events that are beyond our control. To not align with life in these situations is a lot like banging your head against a brick wall repeatedly. No matter how much you wish the wall wasn't there, it still hurts when you whack it.

I love what author and teacher Byron Katie says about aligning with life: "Every time I argue with reality I lose . . . but only 100 percent of the time."

The good news is that I have more than forty-five years of personal experience that the following statement is truth: The unexpected events of life are not here to punish us; they are here to evolve us.

Whether it is a death, a sudden loss of a job, or a broken wrist, it is actually the things that radically rearrange our world in shocking ways that in the long run give us our depth and power. These endings are as important as our beginnings. Death is as sacred as life. Loss creates space for the new to emerge.

Of all the many things that are out of your control, there is one beautiful thing you can have control over: your own reactions. Or at least your reaction to your reactions. As you learn to let go, you'll be able to witness your reactions and guide yourself in a gentle, firm way to shift from unconscious reaction to clear response.

The following exercises are designed to help you align with life, especially in the moments when it's not so easy to do so.

Exercises

2.1 Mantra Practice (Part 1)

Mantra is a Sanskrit word meaning "a sacred saying or phrase that is designed to foster spiritual growth."

Mantras are short prayers to help the mind get quiet and stay focused on the Divine. They're mini-prayers that you say over and over again. If our intentions are pure, prayer can be really helpful when it comes to letting go of something that is causing us pain or anxiety.

I have a specific mantra for when I am frustrated with someone else's actions that helps me to open my hands when I want to clench tight. When I notice myself wanting someone else to be or act differently, I breathe and start my mantra practice:

> They have a right to choose their actions. They are free to make their own choices. They have a right to

choose their actions, even if I don't like it. They are free to make their own choices, even if I don't agree with them . . .

The key to this mantra working is in my willingness to keep moving through my own resistance, justification, and stories to find the truth in it. Remember, a mantra is not a magic pill ("Say this four times and call me in the morning."). A mantra is more akin to sandpaper that helps us smooth off the rough edges of our own self-inflicted "things should be different than they are" misery.

To work the mantra for yourself, think about a situation in your life where you want someone else to be different than how they are. Pick one person who is "causing you grief"—your teen-age daughter who you suspect is doing drugs, your ex who is not following the agreements you made, your insensitive boss, or your nosy neighbor and her yappy dog. Now repeat the mantra in the previous paragraph with that person in mind.

Now, here is the important question: Are you willing to work the mantra and let it smooth off your rough edges? This means you have to be willing to believe the mantra *more than you believe your own story.* You must be willing to release the mental position of "they should," and respect their right to choose their own actions. And you must be willing to align with what life is bringing in this moment.

2.2 Mantra Practice (Part 2)

Aligning with life does not mean we passively accept everything around us no matter what. If there's a situation that you want to change, and it is within your power to either change it yourself or ask that it be changed, then it is perfectly fine to do so. In fact, for many of us, making such changes falls under the category of speaking our truth (see Lesson 8).

Being a Warrior Goddess is about having the wisdom to know what we have choice over and what is beyond our control. Here is an example: I once had a coaching client who was frustrated that her neighbors were playing loud music late into the evening. "I've tried everything!" she told me. "I've prayed, forgiven them, surrounded my house with light . . ." She was very upset, losing sleep regularly, and having recurring trouble at work because she couldn't do her job effectively.

I almost didn't ask the following question because I assumed she had already done so, but something inside told me to confirm. "Sweetheart, did you go knock on their door and let them know the impact their music was having on you and see if they could turn it down?" I asked.

"No," she replied, as she looked at me with surprised eyes. "Is that an okay thing to do?"

Warrior Goddesses, remember it is always okay to ask that a need you have be met. Just remember that your asking may or may not lead to a change in the other person's behavior. (When it doesn't, see 2.1 Mantra Practice (Part 1).) But whether your asking brings about the desired change or not, speaking up about it will help you to be clear about your own choices and creative in your responses to life.

Here is the mantra to practice to help you find and align with your choices, find your deepest truth, and engineer a creative response to what is before you. The next time you are in a situation that is causing you suffering, say the following mantra:

What is my choice? What action can I take? Who do I want to be in this situation? What is my choice? What action can I take? Who do I want to be in this situation?

As you repeat your mantra, keep moving beneath the stories that keep you trapped in the mindset of victimhood. What is your choice? What action can you take? Keep asking, and the answers will materialize within you. Finally, when you are in those situations where no effective action is possible, can you align with the present moment and accept things as they are? When you do, who you become in the situation is peace.

2.3 Clear Alignment

The Mantra Part 2 practice is a great corollary to this Clear Alignment practice from *Warrior Goddess Training*. Use this technique to gain clarity, and then hold it up to the light of current reality to help navigate your everyday choices.

What do you really want in a given situation? Sometimes it's easy to answer this question, and sometimes it's hard to know for sure. Start being proactive in getting to clarity by asking yourself, "What do I want now?" regularly throughout your day. Then connect this clarity with awareness of what is happening now and what is possible.

In just four simple steps, you can navigate any situation, simple or complex:

1. Get **clarity**: Ask yourself what you want.
2. **Reality** check: Look at what is actually true and present in the moment.
3. Get greater **clarity**: Ask yourself again what you want.

4. Make your best **decision**: See what you can align to in this moment.

Here's an example: I get quiet and listen to my body, and I feel that I want Thai food for lunch instead of the hamburger that someone offered to pick up for me (clarity). But I'm on deadline and do not have time to get Thai food (reality). So I ask again, "What do I want?" and I realize that I want something light (clarity). So I opt for the salad bar at the deli next door (decision).

2.4 Review the Past

One exercise that can help us remember the benefits of aligning with life is to review the past.

Looking back over your life, what experiences were painful at the time but ultimately led you to a better place or provided you with other gifts? Divorce, the death of a loved one, or losing a job is often fertile ground for exploration. Remember, aligning with life doesn't mean that you would have chosen the situation; it just means that in hindsight you can see how there were gifts that came from it as well.

Past Painful Situation:	How I Felt at the Time:	Ultimate Gifts:

Are you in a tough situation right now? Going forward, can you anticipate what gifts you could ultimately gain as you transition from this difficult time?

2.5 One Thing a Day: Surrendering Practice and Prayer

Learning to let go takes practice! A great way to begin this sacred art is to part with some material possessions. (It's no coincidence that many spiritual traditions suggest a paring down of unnecessary goods, as one benefit is to learn the art of surrender.) I suggest that you start small. Is there anything in your house that doesn't bring you joy or serve a purpose? Donate these things to a thrift store or give them to a friend. Give away clothes that don't fit you or that you haven't worn in a year. Notice how you feel lighter on the inside by practicing the art of letting go on the outside.

Clearing out unwanted possessions is just the first step. What other things is it time to let go of? Perhaps a relationship that no longer serves you? Are you committing to obligations that no longer fulfill you? Notice all the places in your life that are asking you to open your hands, and let go. This will help when the bigger life circumstances, like the ending of relationships, or aging, or changes at work, come up and require the art of surrender.

Make a list of the things you would like to surrender. I suggest starting with material possessions, and then adding unhealthy behaviors, any over-commitments you have made, or relationships that no longer serve you. Lastly, perhaps you can surrender the desire that a specific person change his or her behavior (see Mantra Practice (Part 1)).

_____

_____

_____

_____

_____

_____

Once you've made your list, reflect on it, and say aloud the following surrender prayer:

> As a Warrior Goddess, it is my desire to surrender these things that no longer serve my highest good. I am willing to release them so that something new and wonderful can emerge in my life.

Additional Gifts

- Beneath all of our stories, projects, and desires, life continues to do what it does. You can fight it, or you can flow with the changes.

- Life is a glorious circle of transformation, each ending a beginning and each beginning an ending.

- Find the sweet spot between total commitment and complete surrender. That is where freedom lies.

- Laughing helps us to not take life so seriously, and realizing how small we are in the mystery of life helps us release our illusion of control.

Lesson

2

Lesson 3

Purify Your
Vessel

From

Warrior Goddess Training

Our first two lessons focused on committing to ourselves and aligning with life. For these two things to work effectively, we must purify what I call our "vessel." This vessel is defined as a sacred container of awareness that holds all of you. Your mind, energy, emotions, and physical body are all part of the vehicle for the spirit, or the invisible essence that is at your core. Your vessel houses your spirit, and your spirit cannot express fully if your vessel is burdened by things that don't serve you.

Specifically, this means we must become aware of and consciously clear out all the beliefs, stories, fears, and general gunk that is clogging our system. And this takes rolling up our warrior sleeves and getting to work while we also open to divine goddess grace and inspiration.

Lesson

3

Warning: Inner cleaning is not for the faint of heart! It takes courage, grit, and some good scrubbing tools, and that's exactly what we will need if we are to purify our vessel.

But before we go further, let's clarify what it means to "purify your vessel" in the context of Warrior Goddess Training.

Purifying your vessel does not mean that you are dirty, or that in order to be "clean, worthy, or perfect" you must reject your current self in exchange for a new, "holier" version. You are already holy, whole, worthy, and perfect.

You are like a river whose source is a crystal clear spring. There may be times when fear, frustration, self-doubt, and other contaminants enter further down the river, but no matter how polluted the water becomes downstream, the source is always pristine. And like the river, regardless of what elements are introduced later, it can always be purified, bringing the water back to its natural state.

Life can be messy. But you are not the beliefs, stories, or fears that are clogging your innate happiness and peace.

And by now you know that true happiness can't be found by buying another blouse; true peace can't be felt by chasing an idea of physical perfection; and true self-acceptance can't be experienced when you try to make everyone else happy at your own expense.

You are on the Warrior Goddess path to claim all aspects of your being, to own who you truly are, and to create the space within yourself to let your natural state of happiness arise. That happiness will come about when you come to love your quirky personality, your love handles, and your mistakes, rather than punishing yourself for being human. The goal of purifying our vessel is to clean out all our self-rejection, self-judgment, and self-comparison, so we can get down to the business of loving ourselves for who we are fully and completely.

Choosing to focus on cleaning does not equate to you being selfish or broken. Internal cleaning is as practical and simple as the everyday tasks you do to maintain the gifts in your life, such as brushing your teeth (Yay, teeth!), vacuuming the floors (Yay, carpets!), or doing laundry (Yay, clothes!). And yay, you! Let's clean!

Exercises

3.1 Create a Container

From *Warrior Goddess Training:*

Our first step in purifying all aspects of self is to learn to be in a relationship with ourselves in a new way by creating our vessel—an imaginary container that keeps us inner-focused and prevents us from becoming hooked into the multitude of opinions and stories that are constantly competing for our attention throughout the day. These could include messages from the media, the opinions of friends, expectations of relatives—all of which can trigger the familiar sabotaging voice of self-judgment and self-doubt.

When you create a strong container of self-awareness around yourself, you stop leaking your inner power through self-criticism, judgment, comparison, and doubt. This container of your presence and self-acceptance needs to be strong to allow the fires of transformation to burn away all that doesn't serve you.

Let's start our purification process by creating an imaginary container that holds you steady during transformation. The following visualization will guide you to create a container that holds all of you in love, and helps to energetically define what is yours versus what belongs to others.

SPHERE OF LIGHT VISUALIZATION

To begin, sit someplace quiet, making sure you won't be disturbed. Get your body comfortable, and read through the visualization a couple times before you close your eyes to do it on your own. Close your eyes, and pick a color that you want to work with that feels healing and energizing. Take some deep breaths, and imagine a flame in the color you chose burning brightly inside your heart. Sit for a few moments, breathing into this heart flame, and feel an abundance of gratitude for your precious life.

Now imagine that a sphere of light, tinted in this same color, surrounds you. This sphere radiates out two feet from your physical body in all directions—it goes under your feet, above your head, in front of, behind, and to the sides of you. This sphere of light is all around you, with no holes or gaps.

This is your container. It defines your energetic body and creates a boundary to hold in and protect your energy from what is not for your highest good. You can imagine it is like a special kind of Teflon: Any energy from the outside that does not benefit you (emotions, thoughts, actions) just rolls off, while any energy

Purify Your Vessel

— 29 —

that will benefit you (love, compassion, inspiration) is able to easily permeate this energetic membrane. Let this container you are imagining be flexible and strong, accessible to the positive but impenetrable to the negative.

Visualize yourself moving through your day, keeping your attention on this container that surrounds you. You can feed and strengthen it with the fire of gratitude in your heart. The more gratitude you have in your heart, the easier it will be to hold your own container.

Now open your eyes and take this container with you as you continue on the path.

Remember, you can use this visualization to recharge the energy of your container at any time. I suggest that you make it a regular practice, perhaps one you do every morning if possible.[1]

3.2 Big Picture Assessment: A Three-Day Practice

The next step is to gain clarity on which areas within you need cleaning. In *Warrior Goddess Training* we touched on these areas briefly, but we are going much deeper here.

I want you to commit the next three days to gathering data about your mind, your energy level, your emotions, and your physical body. The key here is to gather information without judgment. In this way, you are like a sacred scientist studying the habits of the most amazing creature you've ever come across: yourself.

I want you to self-inventory by answering the questions that follow at the end of every day, or throughout the day if you can. I encourage you to write down what you find in your notebook.

---

1   Please visit www.warriorgoddessaudio.com to download a free extended audio version of this exercise.

Something magical happens when we take the time to record things on paper. Patterns and other details become apparent that would not otherwise if we were to keep all of our observations in our head.

Naturally, these four areas will cross over one another in many cases, as they are all a part of the wonderful being that is you.

MIND EXPLORATION

Notice the internal chatter that fills your mind throughout the day. What are the themes you hear most? What are the internal stories that seem to repeat themselves? Does your mind spend more time in judgment about how things should be (including yourself!), rather than in gratitude for the way things are? Notice the ratio of negative versus positive thoughts, and the balance of thinking about the past or future versus being in the present. When and how often do you have stretches of silence and mental quiet? When is your mind at peace?

ENERGY EXPLORATION

Watch your energy levels throughout the day. When do you feel most energetic? When and why do you lose energy? Do specific interactions with others increase or decrease your energy? What thoughts increase or decrease your energy? When and in what circumstances do you feel energetically bright? When do you feel dim?

EMOTIONS EXPLORATION

What emotions do you feel throughout your day? What is your relationship with your emotions? Do they flow, or do you feel stuck? Do you fight and deny your emotions? If so, which ones? How much fluidity and openness do you have emotionally? Are you able to release emotions cleanly and move on? Or do they cycle? How stagnant or volatile is your emotional body? Do you overreact to situations? (Remember, a reaction can be internal or external.)

PHYSICAL BODY EXPLORATION

How does your body feel throughout the day? Does your body feel healthier at certain times of the day? Why might this be so? Are you really in your body, or do you live in your mind? Do you listen to your body's needs? Do you love and respect your physical body, or do you mentally judge your physical form? How do you feel about your body's weight? Do you feel at peace or judgmental about the age of your body? How do you feel when you eat certain foods? Drink alcohol? Or take mood-altering drugs (prescription or otherwise)?

TAKE A THIRD-PERSON PERSPECTIVE

After the three days are over, review your notes and write any patterns you noticed in your notebook. But instead of writing in the first person, answer in the third person, and be as specific as you can. So instead of writing "I spent a lot of time worrying about the future," I would write "HeatherAsh spends about 55 percent of her day worrying about the future." Writing in the third person will free you up to bypass your editor or old ways of perceiving yourself, and also help you get more concrete information.

Now that you have gathered information about these areas, where do you think you need some internal cleaning? Where do you judge yourself, reject yourself, or compare yourself to others? As we move through the lessons in this book, it's helpful to know which areas of your life need attention, so you can bring fierce compassion and self-love to these places, healing yourself in the process.

3.3 Recognize Your Inner Judge and Victim (Part 1)

Much of *Warrior Goddess Training* is devoted to spotting the voices of your inner judge and victim, and learning how to recognize these voices for what they are: fearful illusions that keep you from living the best life possible.

As I wrote in *Warrior Goddess Training*,

> Your inner judge, or critic, is constantly looking for what you or others are not doing right. Your judge doesn't just have high standards; it has impossible standards. Nothing you do is right. Sometimes the judge keeps its focus on what it perceives to be your fatal flaws, sometimes it turns its eye to those around you. Either way, when you listen to the judge's voice as a source of wisdom, you are caught in comparison and frustration.
>
> Your victim, or the I-can't-do-it-I'm-not-enough part of you, is always looking to a judge for validation, which it never gets. The victim will always seek out a judge, whether internal or external, to prove its unworthiness. When you listen to the victim's voice as the truth, you spend your days feeling powerless and without hope.

Sometimes the voices of your inner judge and victim are easy to spot, such as when we judge or victimize ourselves based on our physical appearance; but in many cases these voices can be sneaky and subtle, making them hard to recognize—especially when they are woven into old stories that we have been telling ourselves for a long, long time.

For example, I have a friend who for years felt inferior in certain situations at work. In general she was happy at her job, and she is very good at her profession, but she noticed that she often felt inferior around certain people in the office. Upon deeper exploration, she realized that all of the people she felt inferior around had college degrees in the field, while she had elected to leave college before completing her degree. And while watching for her judge in an interaction with one of them, she heard the internal voice say in regards to her coworker, "You're inferior to her because she went to college . . . You should have listened to your parents and stayed in school."

Another woman I know has done years of personal work, yet she would hear a subtle voice of victimization around the breakup of her first marriage. She witnessed this voice during certain songs, scenes in movies, or other situations where marital infidelity was referenced. She noticed how these situations still left her feeling angry and upset even though the events they reminded her of had taken place many years earlier. She also noticed the same feelings when around her friends who had been married for many years to the same person, because a voice inside her would say, "Your first husband ruined your chance for a long-term marriage because he left you for another woman." And while it may be true that her previous husband was unfaithful, it was the continuous replay of her victim story that was causing her suffering in her current life, keeping her trapped in the negative emotions of the past.

In this lesson, we're focusing on identifying the voices of our internal judge and victim. In the next lesson, we'll use this insight to release and rewrite our old stories. In this exercise, you're going to list the areas in your life where the judge and victim voices speak up, sometimes in sneaky and subtle ways. Write down how they do so either in the space provided below or in your notebook. Some popular topics for the judge and victim are body size and physical features, relationships with partners, parents, siblings, and children, as well as your career.

My judge likes to speak up on the following topics:

_____

_____

_____

_____

_____

My victim likes to speak up on the following topics:

_____

_____

_____

_____

_____

Purify Your Vessel

Noticing the voices, or your judge and victim, is the first step to recognizing them for the fearful illusions that they are. Remember, you are whole, perfect, and loveable exactly the way you are. There is nowhere you need to go, nothing you need to do, and no one you need to be. You are more than enough.

3.4 Clean General False Core Beliefs

Many of our internal judge and victim voices have spoken so loudly and for so long that general false core beliefs arise as a result. Beliefs such as "I am not loveable," "I am not a good person," "I am not worthy," or "I never do anything right" have plagued most of us at some point.

In your journal, I invite you to identify and list your false core beliefs. Take each one individually: On a blank page, write the false core belief as the title at the top. Then, make a list of how this false core belief makes you feel.

Next comes the fun part: cleaning up the lies that spread from false core beliefs like muddy footprints on a clean floor. Start writing down examples of how your false core belief is *not* true. Anytime you remember or experience a truth that is opposite of your false core belief, you wipe a part of that false belief clean. As you start to name the opposites and break the pattern of believing your false core belief, you will also see what cleaning action will help you dissolve the dirt even more.

Here is an example:

False core belief: I am not worthy of love.

This belief makes me feel: sad, depressed, unlovable

Here's how this belief is not true:

- I am a very caring person. I often help others.
- I honor my friendships and relationships by always doing my best.
- Everyone, all beings, are worthy of love, and this includes me.

3.5 Clean Specific False Core Beliefs

Other types of false core beliefs can be very specific and just as self-limiting. Old ideas can remain unquestioned for so long they become accepted as facts. "That's a man's job," "Good girls don't behave that way," or "If he really loved me, he would marry me" are specific false core beliefs that can keep us from experiencing the freedom and happiness we deserve.

Let's consider another example. Jeannette was frustrated because she wanted to marry her partner, but he was resistant to the idea. He had spent years taking care of his parents who had Alzheimer's. He knew that Alzheimer's was often hereditary, and he wanted to spare Jeannette from feeling that she should take care of him if he got the disease later in life. His solution was to not marry. Jeannette found herself feeling that he didn't love her, that he was being silly, and that if he really wanted to be with her, he would marry her. Their relationship suffered.

One day, Jeannette realized that she was causing herself a lot of pain by equating love with marriage. She started questioning why she wanted to be married so badly. What did it mean? She realized that her relationship was wonderful, and that it wasn't marriage she valued, but rather the relationship she already had with her partner. As soon as she let go of her own internal false belief that she had to be married in order to be happy, she realized the truth: She was already happy. She really didn't need to be married; that was an old core belief she had picked up from fairy tales and the media. She also realized that it was her partner's deep love for her that was causing his behavior, not his lack of love. With this new, cleansed perspective, Jeannette was free to love her partner and their relationship fully.

Purify Your Vessel

— *37* —

Are you holding on to any specific false core beliefs? In the space below or in your notebook, list any specific false core beliefs that you have and how they have kept you from experiencing life in the fullest way.

Specific false core belief:

What this specific false core belief has kept me from experiencing:

What would be available to me if I released this false core belief:

_____

_____

_____

_____

_____

_____

Additional Gifts

- You are a most creative, fabulous, and gifted story-teller. Now, what will you do with your powers?

- Stop letting your judge tramp mud across the white carpets of your being.

- Visualize and claim yourself as a divine expression of the Warrior Goddess of the heart.

- Each aspect of your whole self—your mental, energetic, emotional, and physical bodies—is sacred. When you wipe away the dirt of your own false beliefs, you reveal the perfection of your authentic mind, body, and spirit.

Lesson 4

Ground Your Being and Free Your Past

From

Warrior Goddess Training

On an energetic level, humans are a lot like trees. A well-balanced tree has deep roots that go into the earth like a grounding rod. A tree's roots are both its stability and its source of nutrition. The deeper and wider the roots, the more resilient and anchored the tree will be, and the more likely it is to survive changes in the environment, such as high winds or drought.

A well-balanced Warrior Goddess also grows deep energetic roots that sink into the earth. When we are grounded in this way, we have faith in our ability to survive in the world. We trust ourselves. We feel safe and held. We are resilient.

Lesson
4

Believe it or not, for most of our time as a species on this luscious planet, humans have lived in harmony with the earth. We treated the earth as our mother, and all plants, animals, creepy crawlies, and winged ones as our relations. Science tells us that humans have been around for six or seven million years, yet it is only in the last two thousand years or so that we have separated ourselves from Mother Earth, seeing her as a resource to be used for our benefit rather than a relationship to honor and cherish. This disconnect has caused damage to our planet and to ourselves.

As women, many of us have treated buying more stuff, yearning for the one "right" relationship, or striving for the "perfect" body as the most important goals in life. Much like the predominant human attitude toward the planet, we use our bodies and our being as a means of getting what we want rather than fostering an intimate relationship with ourselves through nurturing self-love. Once on the Warrior Goddess path, we realize that true happiness can only be found within, and it is the result of living in harmony with our surroundings and ourselves.

The first part of Lesson 4 is devoted to helping you reconnect to the mother we all have in common, as well as the relationship you have with yourself.

Exercises

4.1 Grounding Meditation and Visualization

In *Warrior Goddess Training,* excerpted above, we explored the important grounding practice of visualizing ourselves as trees with roots going deep into the earth. Let's go deeper now by making this grounding practice a meditation and visualization. Read over the following practice a few times and then try the meditation immediately afterward.

Find a quiet space where you can be alone and undisturbed for the next few minutes. If you can find a quiet place outside underneath a tree, that's even better! Sit comfortably on the ground or in a chair with your spine straight and your belly relaxed.

Close your eyes and take a few deep breaths into your belly; keep softening and opening your abdominal muscles as you breathe in and out. Visualize your breath running up and down the length of your spine as you inhale and exhale. Next, imagine your spine elongating into a taproot, and visualize it traveling down into the earth beneath you.

As you inhale and exhale, imagine your taproot going down into the earth, sinking down through soil. Use all your senses to make it as real as possible: What does the soil smell like? How do your roots feel sinking through the earth? What is the sound of your taproot pushing deeper? What does the soil taste like? The more you use your senses, the more real it will become.

Now imagine that from your taproot more roots sprout and start sinking down and spreading out into the earth. Feel yourself deeply anchored to earth through your roots. Imagine these root sprouts wrapping around rocks or crystals buried deep in the earth, connecting you to the earth even further.

Spend a few minutes breathing into your roots and letting your energetic and physical body reconnect to Mother Earth. When you are ready, slowly open your eyes and notice how you feel.

Whenever you feel yourself getting pulled emotionally or energetically off-balance throughout the day, remember that you can reconnect your being by visualizing your roots anchored strongly into the ground. Because these are energetic roots, they can easily travel with you as you move through your day![2]

4.2 Anchor Adjustment

STEP 1: NAME CURRENT ROOTS

From *Warrior Goddess Training:*

> Many women believe that in order to be safe we have to send our roots and our sense of value into impermanent things: our partner, our children, our youth, our job. We define ourselves and find a sense of being worthwhile by our connection to others. We don't have a central taproot that connects us to a healthy, grounded self. Our entire self-definition gets wrapped in roles like mother, wife, businesswoman, healer, or daughter, rather than our Warrior Goddess divine female essence.
>
> • What people, places, and concepts are you rooting into to feel grounded, safe, and steady?
> • On the next page is a drawing of a tree with five roots going into the earth. Write down the top five roles, people, places, things, and concepts you are anchoring to. Here are some examples of what you might be rooting into to feel a sense of stability and worthiness:

---

2   Please visit www.warriorgoddessaudio.com to download a free extended audio version of this exercise.

- Romantic partner: husband/wife/lover/girlfriend/boyfriend
- Career or vocation (including going to school)
- Past achievements
- Physical appearance (current or past)
- Financial worth or socioeconomic status
- Health
- Pets
- Homemaking
- Parenting
- Volunteering
- Spirituality

What I Am Rooting into Now

Now, label each root from one to ten, according to how strongly you are attached to it, with one being the least attached and ten being the most attached. Don't think; just let the answer arise from within you.

Next, write down how these current attachments have caused you to suffer. Of course, not everything is negative, but right now we are exploring what is not working.

Here are some examples:

- Rooting into my job can lead to perfectionism and controlling behavior at work.
- Rooting into my marriage can lead to overdependence on my spouse.
- Rooting into my physical appearance can lead to self-judgment, especially when I look in the mirror.
- Rooting into my daughter's success can lead to me trying to control her decisions.
- Rooting into my cancer diagnosis can lead to me feeling broken or like I did something wrong.

The Negative Impacts of Rooting into Impermanent Things:

1. _____

_____

_____

_____

_____

2. _____

_____

_____

_____

_____

_____

3. _____

_____

_____

_____

_____

_____

4. _____

_____

_____

_____

_____

_____

5. _____

_____

_____

_____

_____

_____

Step 2: Create a Strong Taproot

One of the goals of *Warrior Goddess Training* is to help you not anchor to the specifics that will change, but to the permanent places like self-love, and your connection to the Divine. When you anchor your roots to something outside of you, you will never feel completely stable. Your beloved, kids, pets, house, parents, work, and friendships will all shift and change, no matter how stable they may appear to be. What can you anchor to that will bring true stability?

Now that you have a map of the way you are staying grounded, let's envision a new way. Start by naming what you want your main taproot to be anchored into. Make it one word: love, presence, compassion, harmony, peace, creativity. You can change this later if you want; for now pick a quality you are wanting to most embody in your life and write it on the taproot in the drawing on the following page.

Now, close your eyes and imagine setting your taproot deep into the earth. Ask Mother Earth for guidance to help you anchor to this new taproot, and support to bring this quality to all of your other roots.

Remember the five things you wrote down as your main roots? Transfer those things to this new drawing. Write a word of your

Lesson
4

intent next to each of them, so that you are choosing to anchor into your own focus and clarity for each of these areas in your life, rather than leaning on them to feel whole.

Here's an example:

Main Taproot: Love

Roots and My New Intent:

- Job—Presence
- Marriage—Partnership
- Physical Appearance—Happy and Healthy
- Daughter—Faith
- Cancer—Temporary

When you name and resonate what you want into the earth through your taproot and then ask for support, the consciousness of the earth and the wisdom of your being start to have a conversation. Keep going back to this taproot and your connection to the earth and listening for guidance.

4.3 Honor All of Creation: A Walking Meditation

Although silent, seated meditation gets most of the attention, there are actually many other ways to meditate. Zen Buddhism, Native American Shamanism, and other spiritual traditions suggest active ways to meditate, such as while chopping wood, drinking tea, or walking a labyrinth, just to name a few. One that I recommend is an outside walking meditation, as this is another great way to stay grounded and to view Mother Earth and all her creations as supporting parts of your family.

The first step of this meditation is to go for a walk outside. It really doesn't matter where outside is for you—it can be into an untamed forest or on a busy street in New York City—this meditation can be done effectively in any setting.

Once outside, stop for a moment to get prepared. Take a few deep breaths and visualize your breath going all through your body, all the way down and into your feet. Feel your feet grounded in the earth, and know the mother is beneath you, and that all around you is family. As you look at your surroundings, imagine that along with all the humans on the planet, every tree, flower, rock, mountain, skyscraper, sidewalk, insect, four-legged animal, and winged animal is your brother and sister. You are never alone, and you are never without guidance. Everything you see is here to support you.

Next, as you begin your walk, be conscious of each step you take. Let it bring you into the present moment. So many times we walk while our minds are someplace else (we're on the phone, thinking about what we have planned for the evening, etc.). But on this walk, your only purpose is to walk consciously, staying aware of your present surroundings.

As you walk, be on the lookout for messages, and remain open to spiritual insights. The wind through the trees might remind you to let your thoughts go on the breeze. The sun shining warmth into your bones is a hug from the sky. The happy dog across the street reminds you to lighten up. Imagine that everything is conspiring to bring you back into the arms of your true family that never left you.

Walk for at least ten minutes in this way, and gradually work your way up to longer periods. When you notice your mind has strayed into what you have planned for tomorrow, or what happened yesterday, don't beat yourself up; instead, gently steer your mind back to an awareness of your surroundings by focusing on each step you take.

4.4 Release Your Old Stories

The second part of Lesson 4 focuses on releasing or rewriting the stories that have kept us grounded in an unproductive version of the past. As human beings, we are storytelling creatures. But if we are not aware, the stories we tell ourselves can become a burden of heavy baggage that we carry around with us from one moment to the next, never realizing we have a choice in what stories we tell ourselves and how they make us feel.

If you did Exercise 3.3 and identified some of your most common judge and victim voices, now would be a good time to review that list. The recurrent voices of our judge and victim are almost always tied to old stories we are telling ourselves that simply are not true.

Here is an example from my own life that I recounted in *Warrior Goddess Training:*

> Example of my old story:
>
> I was traumatized as a child by how often my family moved. I went to eight different schools and lived in four countries—Singapore, Hong Kong, the United States, and Thailand—by the time I was sixteen. We would move every two years or so. I started off at each school feeling painfully shy, disconnected, and alone. By the second year I would have made friends and found my groove, and then we would move again and the cycle would start over. Because of the many times I moved away from friends, or they moved away because of their parent's jobs, I have a hard time connecting with people intimately and I'm afraid of being abandoned.

Now it's your turn. Think about the stories you have told yourself about past life events that caused you suffering. Most of us don't have to dig too deep for these, as they tend to reside in the forefront of our mind. Your story may have to do with your family, a current or past relationship, your career, body or health issues, your children (or lack thereof), etc. Write one or two of your old stories down in the space provided below or in your notebook.

Next, we are going to consciously rewrite your story by changing the perspective: We're going to view your past experience as something that ultimately served your highest good. Following is the rewrite of my story from *Warrior Goddess Training*. Notice that it's the same events, but now seen in a completely different light.

> Example of my new story:
>
> I was blessed as a child with an adventurous family. We moved every two years and traveled around the world every summer. I spent most of my childhood going to great international schools in Southeast Asia, and by the time I was sixteen my family had visited or lived in twenty different countries, including Thailand, Singapore, India, Egypt, Italy, and Spain. Because of the many times we moved and traveled I learned to be incredibly flexible and to deeply love the diversity and creativity of humans. My childhood experiences helped me relate to many different perspectives, to make friends easily, and to celebrate change.

Now it's your turn. I realize that this second part may be more difficult than writing your old story, because that's the one you've been telling yourself and everyone else for a long time. If you are stuck here, one way to start is by listing some good things that have come out of the events you described. (For example, my family moved constantly as I was growing up. This was tough for me, but I later realized it was an opportunity for me to experience many different cultures and perspectives.) Write down your new story in the space provided below or in your notebook.

_____

_____

_____

_____

_____

_____

_____

_____

_____

_____

_____

4.5 Own Your Family Story

Most of us have some deep-rooted story about our family that needs examination and releasing. These stories revolve around traits and behavioral patterns that we have consciously or unconsciously adopted. Begin noticing with curiosity what energy and actions may have traveled down your family lines to you. The best place to start is from a place of gratitude. Separate out your judgment and emotions around your family to simply honor what positive modeling you did get.

THE GOOD STUFF

Take a few moments to write down the things you appreciate about your upbringing. Make a list for each parent or major caregiver of at least five things you appreciate. Here is what I brainstormed for my parents:

Mom:

- Her courage
- Her willingness to travel
- Her ability to put up with my father when he is grumpy
- Her love of horses
- Her love of humans and the many ways she has volunteered and made a difference in people's lives

Dad:

- His incredible will
- His vision
- His competitive joy in playing racket sports
- His financial support so we could travel all over the place
- The many times he came and watched me compete in track

Now it's your turn. Write up to five things you appreciate about the primary figures that raised you in the space below or in your notebook.

_____

_____

_____

_____

_____

_____

THE NOT-SO-GOOD STUFF

Now let's look at five things you took on that you would like to release. What beliefs did your parents or caregivers hold that you still act from unconsciously? What did you take on then that you can release now?

Be willing to look at yourself and your behaviors and see where you picked them up. Some may be blatant, while others may be subtle. Here is my list of patterns I've carried on from my parents:

Mom:

- Her armoring
- Her shyness
- Her belief that she had to take care of others and not herself
- Her nitpicking at others
- Her sense of guilt

Dad:

- His stubbornness
- His going silent when he was upset with someone
- His need to be right
- His desire to distract
- His desire to control situations

Take some time with this. Write up to five things you have adopted that you would like to release in the space below or in your notebook:

_____

_____

_____

_____

_____

_____

_____

_____

The key to releasing old family patterns is to recognize that they are simply passed down unconsciously, and now you are becoming conscious of them. Bless them. Then feel into what you need to do in your life to create a sense of stability and rootedness that is not based in your family patterns.

4.6 Honor Your Ancestors

While it is fairly common to honor or even talk to immediate family members who have passed on, the idea of connecting with long-gone ancestors, especially ones we didn't know or like when they were alive, is not a high priority for many modern women. From a Warrior Goddess point of view, we welcome all resources, in all forms. This sometimes takes a little brain rewiring. We have to let go of believing that the only insight or guidance relevant to us comes from the living, and also have a willingness to forgive and choose to look for the good in those who have passed. Most of us are open to the idea that those who have passed are watching over us, but let's not forget the generations that came before them.

4.7 Create an Ancestral Altar

One beautiful way to honor your ancestors is to create an ancestral altar. This is a place to honor your ancestors and send them your gratitude for your life. Things you can bring to your altar include pictures, candles, family heirlooms or objects, family crests or cloths, flowers, or things you love from nature. You can also make an altar specifically for one family member who loved and supported you. Sit at this altar for a few minutes today and listen to what guidance or wisdom comes through.

Additional Gifts

- Safety comes from connecting to the ancient wisdom and child-like curiosity that lives in your cells. Everything is conspiring to love you, exactly the way you are.

- Put down the old, heavy baggage of your parents' agreements and fears. You don't have to carry anything from the past that doesn't serve your present.

- Choose to honor and shine the gifts of your ancestors.

Lesson

4

Lesson 5

Energize Your Sexuality and Creativity

From
Warrior Goddess Training

Your sexual energy is also your creative energy. You can use sex to reproduce, a most creative act. You can also take the fiery energy of your sexuality and channel it into catalyzing and birthing anything, from books to careers, health to spiritual practice. At its core your sexual energy is your creative flow, and when you choose to channel it, everything becomes your art.

Lesson
5

I've never met a Warrior Goddess who wasn't sexy.

I'm not talking about sexy in terms of what she's wearing or how her body looks on the outside—because Warrior Goddess sexy is all about how you feel on the inside. It's about being in touch with your inner fire. When you feel shiny, sassy, and sparkly *sexy* it shows! This inner fire is ignited when you are in touch with your wants and desires, and have released any self-judgment or inhibiting stories you have told yourself about sex.

The Warrior Goddess woman walks a path of passion for the sake of passion alone, honoring her sexual nature and healing any beliefs that dampen her sexual energy in the process.

This is what I want for you, too.

Feel daunting? I know this is one of the most difficult lessons for many women. But I believe it is because we've been trained to look at our sexuality from the outside in. We are rarely supported to feel into our sexual flow as the inner life force that nourishes us with vitality and healing warmth. The exercises in this workbook are designed to help you do exactly that.

Remember these words from *Warrior Goddess Training:*

> Whether you are celibate, partnered, or have many lovers, reclaiming and healing your relationship to your sexuality is one of the biggest gifts you can give yourself . . .

Your sexual energy is also your creative energy. You can use sex to reproduce, a most creative act. And you can also take the fiery energy of your sexuality and channel it into catalyzing and birthing anything, from books to careers, health to spiritual practice. At its core your sexual energy is your creative flow, and when you choose to channel it, everything becomes your art.

Exercises

5.1 Find and Release Your Sexual Myths

To clear away the many myths about sexuality we learned growing up, let's first expose them to the light of day, and then shed what doesn't serve us like an old skin, so we can grow into our unique sexual flow and expression.

This exercise is in three parts: The first is a writing exploration, the second brings in movement, and the third returns to writing. Working with our body through movement helps us to feel and then release what the body is holding, which might not show up in the writing.

Note: If you have experienced sexual abuse or have any trauma or fears around your sexuality, please do Exercise 5.2: Clear Your Womb first. It's very important that you take it slow, and be extra gentle with yourself as you work on revealing and removing your sexual myths.

And a reminder for all of us: The myths we hold about sexuality (consciously or unconsciously) originated with other people. You don't have to continue to carry them forward and dampen your energy and vibrancy. Your sexuality, passion, creativity, life flow, and yumminess belong to YOU, and only you get to choose how you want to hold or express them, and with whom. Let's begin.

Part 1: Write It Out

First, I want you to list every agreement you can think of that you learned about sex growing up. Also list any agreements you made based on your own experiences. Don't think; just let yourself write as many things as you can. They don't even have to make sense to you! Here is my own list:

> Good girls don't have sex before marriage; only whores do that.
>
> Sex is not to be enjoyed by women; sex is for the enjoyment of their partner.
>
> If I have sex with someone, I need to marry them and stay with them for life.
>
> Women are supposed to be quiet and submissive during sex.
>
> If my partner wants something sexual that I don't like, I need to do it anyway.

Now it's your turn. Write your list in the space below or in your notebook:

_____

_____

_____

_____

_____

_____

_____

_____

_____

_____

_____

Next, read your list out loud. Notice which agreements still resonate with you and which seem silly or untrue.

See all these agreements as the basis for an old story that was written for someone else. Write out this mythological story in the past tense, imagining that you are bringing it fully to light so you can release it.

Remember, there are likely positive, fabulous sexual experiences that you had along the way too, and things you learned that were helpful and supportive of your sexuality. Those are all good, so we will weave them into the new story later. For now, just focus on what you learned that was not supportive to release it through your awareness.

Here is my example based on my list:

Lesson

5

In my old world, the myth was that sexuality was bad and dirty. I wasn't supposed to enjoy it, and if I did I was supposed to be ashamed. If somebody did something to me that I didn't like, I was supposed to be quiet and pretend it was all fine. It wasn't okay for me to ask for what I wanted, or to ask for something different. What was important was to please whomever I was with. My sexuality was not for me, but for the enjoyment of the other.

Now it's your turn. Write out your old myth on a separate sheet of paper, *not in your notebook or in this workbook*. You'll understand why as we move into the next part of the exercise.

PART 2: MOVE AND RELEASE

Once you've written your old myth on a separate sheet of paper, walk around the room and read pieces of it out loud while exaggerating the old agreements with your movements. So you might say, "I had to stay quiet even if I didn't like it!" or "I had to be timid and reserved because sexuality is bad!" "Because I liked sex, I thought I was a whore!" Be dramatic, and be sure to speak the old agreements out loud, perhaps even finding a gesture that goes with each statement. The point is to get in touch with those old agreements so you can feel the release.

When you have walked around and expressed for a few moments, stop and close your eyes and notice how you feel. Notice where in your body you hold the tension of these old agreements.

Then, shake your body from head to toe. Shake off the old patterning, imagining it breaking up and falling to the earth where the old energy is composted and transformed. You might want to put a great song on and dance to release and clear.

Next, burn the old letter (in a safe way, such as in a barbeque pit or fireplace) or rip it up into tiny pieces, letting your body know that you are letting the past false beliefs go.

Now comes the fun part. To reclaim your true sexual integrity and power, think about what agreements you want to hold. What is your truth? Visualize yourself as a sexually full and powerful Warrior Goddess. What does it feel like to love your sexuality? Put on some great music and move around the room, letting your body express itself as you say out loud your new statements: "I

Energize Your Sexuality and Creativity

— 65 —

am a sexual being and I love it!" "I love my fire!" "I claim my sexy self!" "I am a creative, passionate, sensual being!" Repeat statements like these as you move around the space. Then let yourself dance with abandon and invite your sexual self to express. This is for you, not anyone else. Claim this vital aspect of yourself. Claim your life force.

When you are done, close your eyes and notice how you feel. Breathe the energy throughout your body. Place one hand on your heart and one on your pubic mound and breathe into both your heart and your genitals. Say, "Yes!" out loud three times.

Part 3: Write Your New Letter

Sit down and write a letter to the self you were, before you were domesticated around sexuality. What would you want this young self to know? What would you want to share with her about how to be in relationship with her sexual life force? Write from your heart and from your womb! Here is my letter to myself:

> Dear younger self,
>
> Inside of you is something really precious, a fire that is just for you. This fire is your creativity and your power. You have an absolute choice of how and when you want to play with this inner fire, and with whom you want to share it.
>
> This fire of your sexuality can burn intense and hot, or warm you sweetly from the inside. Explore it. Your sexuality is one of the gifts of being human, a pathway to pleasure, connection, release, and love. Remember always that it belongs to you, and that you choose when and how to share it.

Some believe sexuality is dirty, something that you should hide or be ashamed or afraid of. Others think sexuality is a way to get what you want: love, money, or status. There is a lot of misunderstanding about sexuality. But other people's ideas or beliefs are just that: their own. You get to make your own rules, your own way around what is best for you.

Learn about your own sexual fire, and what you like. Remember that your desire is beautiful, and pleasure is sacred. Touch yourself, explore. What kinds of touch do you like? Which parts of your body like which kinds of touch? What brightens your fire?

Just because you feel desire or the heat of your fire burning brightly does not mean you need to act on it. Just because someone wants you to be sexual does not mean you have to. Always, always, always remember that you have a choice. Give yourself the gift of sharing your fire only with those who deeply respect you, want to know what you like, and are fun to be around.

Play. Listen to yourself. Go slow. Take your time. Let the heat build. Use your fire not just as an expression through sexuality, but also take the energy and channel it into exploring art, drawing, writing, cooking. Your fire is your passion for life. Let it burn brightly with you, and don't be afraid of this sacred power. Honor yourself and your sexual fire with gratitude and love, and let it be a pathway to more openness, beauty, and connection in your life.

All my love,

HeatherAsh

When you are done with the letter, put it in an envelope and place it someplace where you can open it up and read it anytime you feel the old story and feelings trying to regain a foothold in your belief system. This letter can remind you of the sacredness and beauty of your sexuality.

5.2 Clear Your Womb

This optional exercise is for those who have experienced sexual abuse or trauma.

In this ritual, you will clean out any energy, thought patterns, or fear you may still be carrying from sexual abuse or trauma. We want to release any heavy energy from the past and replace it with a sacred honoring of your womb and genitals.

For this ceremony you will need some red or pink roses (or any type of flowers will do), a lighted candle, and a bowl of water.

Place the bowl of water, the vase of roses, and the candle in front of you. As you light the candle, invite in the energy and support of the women you love. These can be women you know personally or women who are role models for you. Also invite in the presence of all the women around the world who have healed from sexual abuse. Ask for their guidance and strength.

Close yours eyes, and imagine washing out your womb (or womb space if you've had a hysterectomy) and genitals with the element of water. You can imagine a river or an ocean flowing through you, or a clear lake that you bring into your inner feminine sanctuary of your vagina, ovaries, and womb. Take your time, looking inside for any heavy energy; dark, stagnant thoughts; or fear. With gentleness and love in your imagination, keep bathing your entire pelvis area with water over and over again. Ask for the water to clear out anything that does not belong to you, and to bring in the clear, healing water of purification.

As you clear out your sexual center, imagine that the bowl of water in front of you is absorbing and holding everything that doesn't serve you. When you feel complete or when you are ready to take a break, pour the water into a sink with running water or flush it down the toilet. See the negative energy leaving and being absorbed and transmuted as it is released.

Rinse out the bowl and bring it back to your altar area. Bless the bowl with the candle by moving it over the flame a few times, then place it in front of you and begin to fill it with rose petals. (Keep one rose to the side with all of its petals.) Visualize the old energy of abuse and trauma being replaced with the beauty, peace, and sweetness of the rose petals. Next, take the last rose, the one you set aside, break off the stem, and place it in the middle of the petals. Imagine all the women you called in at the beginning of this ceremony witnessing you and sending you their love and support as the old energy is replaced with the new.

In conclusion, say the following healing prayer out loud:

> My womb is now clear, it belongs to me, and I am free
> to express my sexuality as I choose.

You may need to do this cleansing meditation several times. Keep coming back to it as many times as necessary to release the old and reclaim your body's sovereignty and sparkle.

5.3 Run Sexual Experiments: Ask for What You Want

One really good experiment to run for Warrior Goddess Training is to ask for and receive what you want. Many women keep themselves feeling safe and under control by giving sexually, but not allowing themselves to surrender to really receiving. If you have a supportive partner, I suggest filling them in on the purpose of this exercise and asking them to participate. If you don't have a partner, use your imagination and creativity to do the following alone.

Make a date where you surrender to receiving (with a partner or with yourself!). Notice if this is easy or difficult for you. Can you allow yourself to receive pleasure without giving anything back? Can you let yourself surrender control and be pushed a bit past your armoring in order to merge more fully with the Divine? Are you able to ask for what you want in the moment?

5.4 Cultivate Your Creativity

The ability to be creative is one of the most important gifts of being human, and what many of us haven't realized is that our sexual energy is also our creative energy. You can take the fiery energy of your sexuality and channel it into catalyzing and birthing just about anything. At its core, your sexual energy is your creative flow, and when you choose to channel it, everything becomes your art!

By definition, being creative involves stepping out of your box to experience something new, and that's exactly what these next two exercises are designed to do: get you thinking and being in new and unexpected ways.

I often do this next practice as a paired exercise in workshops. It works great when done alone, but it is even more expansive with a creative friend.

Pick an issue you are working on, and play with new solutions. Start by breathing into your lower belly and calling in some life force creative energy. Then, brainstorm at least five creative solutions to your problem. Don't think, edit, or backtrack—just write. It's okay if some of your ideas aren't realistic. In fact, the more outrageous you allow your ideas to be, the more your brain will open to come up with creative solutions that will support you.

Here are a couple creative brainstorming examples. You'll see that some creative brainstorms are simple and straightforward, while others are more on the wild side. Write down all of your ideas, no matter how outrageous, then review the list for possible actions.

Remember: The great thing about this practice is that just the process of writing down possible creative solutions, no matter how wacky, will open your brain to continue looking for the answer that is right for you. So don't get discouraged if you don't see the immediate answer as you write. You're getting the wheels in motion, and the right answer will come as you continue to engage your creativity and your willingness to find a new solution.

Now, don't think—just write and see what comes out.

> Problem: I'm not happy in my job/in my marriage/in my life/with my children/with my belly, etc.
>
> Creative brainstorm:
>
> - Every morning before I go to work, I'll write down four things I like about my job.
> - Quit my job and move to the Bahamas to sell tacos on the beach.
> - Have someone place a spell on all my coworkers so they are nice to each other.
> - Spend some conscious time each week getting to know a coworker.
> - Talk to my boss to ask for a new position.
> - Give everyone at work a copy of *The Four Agreements*.

- Take a yoga class at lunch or after work to relieve stress.
- Walk at lunch.
- Explore what agreements/stories I'm holding that are making me unhappy.

Problem: My child just started college, and I don't know who I am now. (Or: I just lost my job/I just retired/I have a chronic illness and don't know who I am now.)

Creative brainstorm:

- Take a painting class.
- Go to college myself.
- Make a list of all the things I used to love to do before I had kids.
- Talk to other women who are living fulfilling lives after their children left home.
- Look at the agreements I've made as a mother and release those that no longer serve me.
- Have a big party/ceremony with my closest friends to honor this transition.
- Call my child neurotically every day so I feel connected.
- Walk out of my house and start a new life.
- Meditate every morning and listen to what my inner wisdom shares.

Now it's your turn. Think of a problem or issue you are currently dealing with, and brainstorm some new and creative ways to deal with it. If you have more than one problem, focus on one at a time, and use separate sheets of paper. It's important that you actually write your ideas down—don't just think about it. There is something cathartic and healing about the act of writing down our thoughts and feelings.

Problem: _____

_____

_____

_____

_____

Creative brainstorm: _____

_____

_____

_____

_____

_____

As you brainstorm both inside and outside the lines, new possibilities will open up. Keep breathing into your belly, connecting to your creative life force, and stretching your brain toward the outrageous. Notice what you typically do, and seek what would be different from your usual pattern. Be creative! The best actions to help you return to integrity come from the wellspring of creativity that you possess. Be playful as you dream up new ways to experiment and take action.

Once you've written down all your ideas, review your list. Perhaps the best course of action is right there in front of you. If it isn't, the process of being able to rule out those ideas will help you narrow in on what you *do* want, and you will probably see a new solution after regrouping.

5.5 Creative Exploration

Pick one creative thing you can do that is unfamiliar, outside your comfort zone, or something you haven't done for a long time, and commit to doing it in the next month. Maybe it's taking a dance class or painting workshop, or building a tree house for your daughter. Don't approach this with the expectation of perfecting whatever it is you do; the goal here is simply creative exploration and having fun. Even if your old story says, "You're not good at those types of things," or the judge says, "Don't even bother trying that," be willing to stretch yourself.

Here's an example of one of my creative explorations: One summer I really wanted an outdoor platform under the trees to meditate on. My partner was traveling, and I almost said, "Well, when he gets back I'll have him make me a platform." But then I got inspired to stretch myself and play with seeing what I could create. I sketched out what I wanted, measured the area, and went out and bought wood. I had to learn how to hold the drill to get the screws in, and I had lots of moments of laughter as I tried to figure out how to make it all fit together. Even though my platform was not perfect, I was so proud of myself for creating it, and I felt empowered to continue to try new things, even if I felt awkward or scared.

Write down one creative thing you want to try (or do again if it's been awhile) and also write down today's date. You have one month to complete this creative endeavor:

_____

_____

_____

_____

_____

Additional Gifts

- The Warrior Goddess claims all of herself, including her sexual fire, and learns how to be warmed by her own inner glow.

- Your sexual life flow is a powerful healing force of nature. It only causes harm if we repress it or force it.

- Your sexual integrity arises from honoring what turns you on as well as how you choose to express and play in the world.

- There is no one "right" way to be with your body and choose how you express your sexuality. Celibacy is a choice, as is having lots of lovers, as is monogamy. None is more enlightened or better than the other. There is only what is right for you.

Lesson 6

Claim Your Strength and Ignite Your Will

From
Warrior Goddess Training

As a Warrior Goddess, your strength is in embracing the challenges of life, loving all of you, including your weaknesses, and saying yes to discomfort. This does not mean seeking out drama or difficult situations, but using everything in your life to foster more resilience, courage, and core strength . . .

If we try to avoid the hard work of breaking down our old confining structures or if we make other people responsible for our own freedom, we will not have what it takes to truly inhabit our essential nature. When we stand in our own center, the challenges we encounter temper us. We can see our inner and external struggles as the cocoon or the wind, the very thing that will strengthen our wings and let our branches reach up to the sky.

Lesson
6

Claiming your strength doesn't mean you become invincible, or that you still won't have fears. On the contrary, claiming your strength is about naming your shadows, befriending them, and turning them into allies. By embracing our vulnerabilities and exploring our fears, we transform them from a constant drain on our energy to our most powerful and nurturing teachers.

How can the vulnerable and scared parts of us also be part of our strength? Doesn't being powerful mean never feeling fear and not naming our weaknesses? Actually, it's just the opposite.

When we try to pretend we are not afraid, we are repressing our fears rather than releasing them. And what we repress doesn't go away; it simply lays in wait for the next time or situation that invites these fears to come out. In everyday language, this is what happens when someone "pushes your buttons"—they've provoked an emotional reaction in you rather than a mature, measured response. To find the source of this reaction, you have to identify the fear hiding underneath it, and bring that fear to the transformative light of day.

A friend shared a similar metaphor with me recently: Ignoring an aspect of ourselves that we fear or that makes us feel vulnerable is akin to trying to hold a beach ball underwater. All your energy and strength goes toward pushing the ball down, but eventually, no matter how hard you try, the ball will come up. The irony is that if you let the ball up to the surface and claim it as yours, you see that it floats away by itself, and only then do you become free of it.

Once you claim your strength, your will is ignited almost simultaneously, as you now posses the courage to stay steady with your heart's desire despite opposition and maintain the clarity of your purpose even when faced with obstacles in your path.

But as you claim your strengths and ignite your will, you need to know what you really want. This will come more easily for those who are already attuned to their heart's desire. For others it may be more difficult—especially if you have put others' needs and wants ahead of your own for a long time. In these cases, getting clear about what you want may take a little more time, and that's okay. Remember to be gentle with yourself on this path of self-discovery.

Exercises

6.1 Transform Fears, Weaknesses, and Vulnerabilities into Strengths and Allies

Now it's time to expose our fears, weaknesses, and vulnerabilities to the light of day, and in the process transform them into allies. The intent of this exercise is not to cover over or pretend you have no weaknesses; rather, it's an invitation to see yourself from a place of power rather than a place of victimization or judgment. From this place of strength and compassion, you can work with your weaknesses and guide yourself to nurture your strengths.

In your notebook or the space provided below, list what you consider to be your fears and weaknesses. Then, in a second column, name how each fear or weakness is also a strength.

Here is my list as an example:

My Fears and Weaknesses	How They Are Also Strengths
I'm afraid of speaking my truth with people close to me.	I am compassionate and do my best to share from the heart.
I want to be liked.	I love humans and am really good at putting people at ease.
I'm not so great at math.	I've learned how to balance my checkbook, and I am great at reading and writing.
I have a hard time paying attention and am easily scattered.	I'm fluid and multitask well.
An old knee injury from a horseback riding accident still bothers me.	I remember to honor my body by slowing down when I transition from sitting to standing.

My Fears and Weaknesses	How They've Made Me Stronger

Claim Your Strength and Ignite Your Will

Once you've finished, create a new column and write down all the things in your life that you have "survived." These things are often our vulnerabilities. Next to each item, write down how each vulnerability has also made you stronger.

Here is my list as an example:

Things I've Survived	How They've Made Me Stronger
Childhood sexual abuse	This helped me be more compassionate and passionate about protecting kids.
Moving around as a kid and feeling shy	Moving around prepared me to travel and speak to new people, and I love airports and hotels.
Losing my dad	I learned how to really show up with my dad at the end, and how to guide others through the loss of a parent or someone close to them.
A difficult divorce	I found my inner strength and resiliency.
Closing down a business I loved	I learned that I can recreate things I love even when I have to let go of the old form.

Things I've Survived	How They've Made Me Stronger

Lesson

6

When we claim all aspects of ourselves, there is no place we can't go, no person we can't face, no task we can't accomplish. Once we have nothing left to hide, we realize that our internal fears and weaknesses are as endearing as our triumphs and successes. In the next exercise, we will look at a new way to move through fear whenever it arises.

6.2 Love Yourself Through Fear and Vulnerability

Pick a time in your life when you felt powerless or afraid. It might be from your distant past or something recent. It might be a big situation or a small one. Be careful not to dismiss writing about a fear or vulnerability because you think it's too minor or insignificant to write about, as it's often through investigating these daily struggles that we get clues about our deepest needs for healing.

What's a situation where have you felt powerless or afraid?

_____

_____

_____

_____

_____

Now, soothe yourself as you would a child. This doesn't mean intellectually talking yourself out of being afraid, or justifying your fears. Soothing is an expression of loving presence. We are not trying to fix or make it better; we are metaphorically holding our own hand, wrapping ourselves up in an embrace, looking ourselves in the eye and saying, "I see you. It is okay. I'm here."

Now ask yourself, Why do I feel vulnerable in this situation? What is my deepest fear? What other fears do I have around the situation?

_____

_____

_____

_____

_____

As you read your answer, continue to soothe yourself with your words and attention until you feel a sense of calmness, accepting yourself where you are in the moment. As you do this, can you notice that the moment calmness and acceptance return is also when your strength flows back in? The situation may not have changed, but now you know you have the internal resources to deal with it.

From this place of peace, ask yourself, what can be your focus in this situation should it reoccur?

_____

_____

_____

_____

_____

Here is a recent example from my life:

As I'm working on this book, I'm also in Peru with a group. I'm wishing I didn't have to divide my attention between my writing and immersing myself in the land and with the group. Part of me thinks, "Oh, Peru is the perfect place to write!" And as I'm writing this, I'm sitting in the hotel restaurant, looking out a huge window to the blossoms, green grass, trees, and water fountain outside. Perfect.

And in my belly I feel tension. So I ask myself the question, How do I feel vulnerable in this situation? What is my deepest fear?

My vulnerability is that I'm not doing it right, that if I were a "committed and real writer," I would have finished the book before I came to Peru.

As I write, tears come to my eyes. So I stop, let them flow, and listen to what other fears or vulnerabilities are present.

This is what arises: I've taken on too much, and I am tired of holding everything together. More tears. I sit quietly with myself, listening, feeling, loving this part of myself, too.

As I sit and self-soothe, I begin to feel more spacious, and I feel my body relaxing. I feel heard. I notice I feel calmer, more centered, and in acceptance of what is. I feel my tiredness and also my tremendous excitement around this book.

My focus: Keep being gentle with myself, keep writing. And when I am not writing, put it down completely so that I can immerse myself in the magic of Peru and be fully present with our fabulous group.

6.3 Discover What You Really Want

From *Warrior Goddess Training:*

Igniting your will occurs when you are clear on what you really want for yourself, and when you take action based on this knowledge. If you are consumed with what others think, you are repressing your fears, and you will not have the will needed to stand in your power.

So the first step to claiming your strength and igniting your will is to get clear about what you want. Not what your victim wants, or what your judge wants, or what you would like, but what your highest vision and purpose is for yourself. What I have found is that when you get clear about your heart's desire, the Universe steps up in magnificent ways to support you!

Let's find out what you really want in life. Write down your answers to the following questions. Don't spend too long thinking about them, or you risk succumbing to the judge or victim. Don't edit as you write—just see what comes through. It doesn't matter if a voice in your head yells, "That isn't realistic!" as you write down your answers; the point here is to let your true desires spill out. If there isn't enough space for your answers below, continue writing in your notebook.

- What do you want your most intimate relationships to look like?
- My response: I want my intimate relationships to be based in honesty, respect, and compassion, and I want to be supportive and loving toward myself, even when I make a mistake.

- Your response:

- What do you want your career to look like? (Remember, raising children is also a big-time job!)
- My response: I want to write a book a year, have a balanced home and travel life, and share the teachings with many people to help foster transformation and open space for more love and creativity in the world.
- Your response:

- What do you want your relationships with your family and friends to look like?
- My response: I want to have the time to play and celebrate with my friends and family.

- Your response:

_____

_____

_____

_____

_____

- What do you want your free time to look like? (Do you want to dance more? Spend more time learning? Travel?)

My response: I want to spend more time singing and in nature. I want to stay steady with my spiritual practices and exercise in a way that makes my body feel strong and healthy.

Your response:

_____

_____

_____

_____

_____

6.4 Explore Core Strategies

As you learn what you really want in life, you might realize that you have actually misused your will up until this point. Most likely, you have learned to use your will for one main purpose: to stay safe. There are many ways we create a (false) sense of safety for ourselves:

- Trying to change and manipulate our environment (*controlling*)
- Bouncing from thing to thing (*distracting*)
- Hiding and pretending to be small (*isolating*)
- Making sure others like us (*pleasing*)

I call these four ways of being our core strategies, and I first wrote about them in one of my first books, *Spiritual Integrity*, with coauthor Raven Smith. Following is a synopsis of how our strategies sap our strength, and how to take back our power.

As women, most of us have a bit of all four strategies working within us. We also tend to have a whole lot of one of them within us. Your *core strategy* is your go-to response. It gives you a sense of power, safety, and stability when you feel scared or confused, and it keeps the world manageable.

Refer to the chart that follows to see how your core strategy is affecting how you react in situations.

Core Strategy	Description
Controller	Controllers feel safe when they are in control of either the world around them or their own internal world. Controllers can be great leaders and visionaries, but often their gift is used to squash uncomfortable situations, to force people to do what they want them to do, and to limit expression. Controllers manage their own and others' emotions through subtle or blatant domination or manipulation. They believe their way is the right way and the only way.
Distractor	Distractors keep themselves safe by staying busy and checked out. Instead of feeling their feelings or facing discomfort, distractors spend hours playing video games, doing projects/hobbies, talking to friends, seeking out anything that can be a distraction! Distractors have a great gift for multitasking and are often mentally nimble, but their energy is easily scattered, and they have a very difficult time focusing and creating what they want in the world.
Isolator	Isolators habitually hide when they are scared or are in an uncomfortable situation. This hiding may be a physical or emotional retreat. When triggered (or before there can be any trigger), isolators head for the safety of the hills. Isolators often have a very strong connection to Spirit and an excellent sense of self, but they are split between a yearning to be deeply seen and understood and a desire to be invisible. They habitually constrict their energy and their choices.
Pleaser	Pleasers believe they will only be accepted and safe when they are helping others. Pleasers constantly scan other people's reactions, wanting to make sure that everyone is happy. Their gifts are sensitivity and an aptitude for sacred service, but when they are in their strategy to keep safe, they become hypervigilant and outer-focused. The result is they often feel victimized and resentful. Pleasers often feel lost when they are not caretaking or acting to satisfy the perceived needs of others.

How do you react to stressful situations? Do you take control, suddenly find something else is more important, isolate yourself, or care take and please others? Look for your core strategy, the one you default to when you are surprised or overwhelmed.

Spend the next few days witnessing your strategy. How does it play out in your life? How does it affect you? Play with being inspired by the brilliance of your strategy, not overwhelmed by its strength. Notice how it has served you in the past, knowing as you gain awareness of the ins and outs of your strategy that you are gaining power over it.

6.5 Experimenting Beyond Strategies
From *Warrior Goddess Training:*

> One of the best ways to release unconscious strategies and do what you really want to do, respond how you really would like to respond, and act as you really want to act is to run experiments to free up your energy. We want to live authentically, not automatically. This is a shift away from the will of our strategy and into the will of our strength.
>
> These types of experiments are similar to what the Toltec call "not doings." A not doing is an action that you take for no reason except to break old patterns. Some simple examples of not doings are eating with your nondominant hand, driving to work a different way each day, or digging a deep hole and then filling it up again. The goal of not doings is twofold: to help you learn to put 100 percent of yourself into an action for no reward or reason, and to shake up habitual ways of being.

Here are a few ideas for not doings. You set the time frame, and away you go! These are not forever actions, but a way to use your will to come into more choice.

- **For controllers:** Form a fast opinion. Don't share your point of view, even when you are asked for it. Go into silence. Make a practice of saying, "I was wrong."

- **For distractors:** Practice regular five-minute focus sessions where you stop and bring your attention to your breath and body. Do one thing at a time. Wait one minute between tasks.

- **For isolators:** Go out to a gathering or event even if you don't feel like it. Set your intent to meet one new person a day. Go deeper with someone you know and trust by sharing a vulnerability.

- **For pleasers:** Say no to any requests you receive that you would usually say yes to. When you are at someone else's house, don't do the dishes or extra work. If someone asks you where you want to have lunch, share your opinion.

Any good experiment around dissolving unconscious strategies is going to be challenging in some way because it will be unfamiliar. Be gentle with yourself. We take on specific strategies often as young children, and it can be surprisingly unnerving when we start to shift away from them. Stay the course, and let the transformation happen.

Lesson 6

Additional Gifts

- Listening to your own guidance is an act of power and presence.
- Practice seeing your fears as an invitation to show up more fully.
- Naming, claiming, and releasing your old strategies frees up energy to choose new possibilities.

Lesson 7

Open Your Heart

From

Warrior Goddess Training

One of the primary heart-armoring beliefs we carry is that people can hurt you. Yes, it is true that your physical body can be hurt. But is your physical body "you"? It is true that your emotional body can be hurt. Is your emotional body "you"? There are many people who are crippled or in emotional pain, but their essence is untouched. If you believe you are only your body or your emotions, you will constantly fear physical or emotional pain. Your armored heart will contract just thinking about the slightest possibility of physical or emotional pain, even if it is not happening! And this is what we spend most of our lives doing, worrying about how we are going to avoid pain and grasping after fleeting pleasures.

When you open your understanding to the wider truth that nothing can hurt the real you, and that you need nothing and no one to be complete, you will feel the unbounded, unchangeable, unified spirit that you are. You will choose what type of relationships to be in not based on fear ("I should be in a relationship by now," "I better get married so I can have kids," "At least it is better than being alone"), but rather from a place of unconditional self-love, where you will intuitively know what would best serve you in this time of your life. No part of your heart will need to close down, because you know that your heart can't be broken.

Lesson

7

When I was younger, love was something I wanted more of, but was often reserved in where and with whom I was willing to share it. I thought that love from the outside, from that "someone special," would fill me up, but I soon found out that the "fix" I felt from the love of another was always temporary, and ultimately left me searching like an addict for the next romantic high.

Once firmly planted on the Warrior Goddess path, I realized there was another way. Love isn't something we bestow on someone when they give us what we want, and withhold later when they don't. Love isn't something we look for in someone else in order to feel complete. As we now know, we are already complete, whole, and powerful just as we are.

But learning to love ourselves can be challenging for many of us at first, as we have spent years being our own worst critic. We can start by giving ourselves the attention we previously craved from others, with a willingness to love every aspect of our being— even the parts we don't like.

We love our quirks, we love our flaws, we love our hips (no matter what size they are), and, most of all, we love our beautiful, open heart. Slowly, your love will permeate all parts of you, until when you are squeezed only love comes out.

Best of all, when we finally begin to love ourselves, we no longer live in a world of fear. This doesn't mean we don't sometimes feel afraid; it just means that fear is no longer dominating our choices.

When we find ourselves, we find love. Love is what we are. This lesson will help you to identify and remove the blocks that have kept you from experiencing the love that you are.

Exercises

7.1 Find the Love Inside You

Find a quiet room where you can sit undisturbed for a few minutes. Close your eyes, and imagine someone or something you deeply love. Hold that image in your mind. If you choose a thing (like your cat or your grandmother's pendant), this item should *not* be in the room with you as you do the exercise.

As you focus intently on this image, notice how you feel. Do you feel the warmth in your belly? Do you feel a sense of lightness? How does love feel? Now integrate your breath. Breathe in and out, imagining that you are nurturing this love with the life force of breath. Do this for the next couple minutes, and anytime you get distracted come back to your heart and the feeling of love.

After two or three minutes of holding this image of love, open your eyes. Isn't the feeling of love wonderful? And did you notice that you are still alone? You have been alone this whole time. This is indisputable proof that you were the cause of the love you felt.

The truth is that while something outside of you might be the catalyst for your love to flow, you are the one creating the love. And if you are the one creating the love, that means you can choose to generate love for the pure pleasure of loving. So why not just choose to love because it feels good to love?

7.2 Recognize Your Inner Judge and Victim (Part 2)

In Lesson 3, we were introduced to the inner judge and victim, and we began to identify their voices. In Lesson 4, we saw that these voices are often tied to stories we tell ourselves, and that releasing and rewriting those stories can quell the voices. Now, we will use the power of self-love and compassion to support ourselves when these fearful voices show back up.

The most intimate relationship you will ever have is with yourself. But if you don't love every aspect of yourself, then your relationship is out of balance. When your inner judge or victim shows up, the path of the Warrior Goddess invites you to love these parts of yourself as well. Compassion is the key to doing so.

In this exercise, you'll identify and write down three examples of when your judge took charge and three examples when your victim led the day. For many of us, these areas are repetitive throughout our lives (relationships, career, family, body image, etc.), as we habitually self-judge or self-victimize over similar types of situations. By writing these down, you can better recognize them for what they are the next time they come up, and consciously acknowledge and release them. This means loving these voices as a part of yourself, but choosing to no longer believe the messages they are telling you.

Here are some examples:

Judge:

- My judge listed all the things that are wrong with me as I skimmed a magazine while waiting for my appointment.
- My judge criticized me for hours about how careless I am when I got a parking ticket the other day.

- My judge got angry with me for having an off day and forgetting to pick up my kid's project after school. It kept telling me what a terrible mother I am.

Victim:

- My victim spent an afternoon making up stories about how everyone in my class had a better child-hood than I did, and how unfair that is.

- My victim felt overwhelmed and scared when I was getting close to my deadline, and kept whining that I wasn't strong enough or loved enough to finish any-thing and that I should just give up.

- My victim keeps reminding me of how scary the world is, and says my only safety is in food.

Now it's your turn.

List three recent examples of your inner judge voice.

1. _____

_____

_____

_____

Lesson

7

2. _____

_____

— *98* —

_____

_____

3. _____

_____

_____

_____

_____

List three recent examples of your inner victim voice.

1. _____

_____

_____

_____

2. _____

_____

*Open
Your
Heart*

_____

_____

3. _____

— 99 —

_____

_____

_____

_____

FROM JUDGMENT TO DISCERNMENT

We've learned that the opposite of judgment is discernment. When we discern, we access the clear wisdom of our mind and our heart working together. Contrast this with how quickly our heart closes when the judge appears in any form. This is how you can tell if you are judging rather than discerning: Your heart will clench. An open "I do not like his behavior," or "That was not your best, dear one—let's try again," is very different than "He is a horrible asshole," or "You blew it again. I knew you would— you can't do anything right."

Here are some examples of the shift we're trying to make from judgment to discernment:

Judgment	Discernment
My judge listed all the things that are wrong with me as I skimmed a magazine while waiting for my appointment.	My new discerning question to ask: What inspired me in the magazine I was reading, and how can I apply this insight to my life?
My judge criticized me for hours about how careless I am when I got a parking ticket the other day.	The ticket was a great reminder to be more aware of my surroundings.
My judge got angry with me for having an off day and forgetting to pick up my kid's project after school. It kept telling me what a terrible mother I am.	I am grateful for my much-needed day off. The next time I have an errand that would be easy to forget, I'll set a timer on my phone. I am a mom who is doing her best.

From Victimization to Compassion

When the heart speaks through discernment there is compassion, which can be gentle and sweet or forceful and direct, cutting to the truth instantly. Compassion is not a passive, no-action place, but a powerful, passionate embrace of life stemming from the heart. To unweave the binds around our heart's wisdom and transition from a judging, closed stance to a present, compassionate opening takes practice. By becoming aware of when you are using your judge internally and externally, you will learn to take new action.

Here are some examples of the shift we're trying to make from victimization to compassion:

Victimization	Compassion
My victim spent an afternoon making up stories about how everyone in my class had a better childhood than I did, and how unfair that is.	I had the childhood I had, and I honor my strength and courage on my healing journey without needing to compare.
My victim felt overwhelmed and scared when I was getting close to my deadline, and kept whining that I wasn't strong enough or loved enough to finish anything and that I should just give up.	It's okay to feel overwhelmed and scared, and I'm dedicated to staying strong and finishing this project.
My victim keeps reminding me of how scary the world is, and says my only safety is in food.	I can trust myself to find safe people and safe environments to nourish me.

Now it's your turn. Using your own inner judge and victim stories, rewrite your answers from a place of self-love.

Judge rewrite: My new discernment perspectives for my examples are:

1. _____

_____

_____

_____

_____

_____

2. _____

_____

_____

_____

_____

_____

3. _____

_____

_____

_____

_____

_____

Victim rewrite: My new compassionate perspectives for my examples are:

1. _____

_____

_____

_____

_____

2. _____

_____

_____

_____

_____

3. _____

_____

_____

_____

_____

*Open
Your
Heart*

7.3 Metta Meditation

There is a beautiful ancient Buddhist meditation called *metta*, or loving-kindness. This is a great Warrior Goddess heart practice that will have a huge impact on your heart. The goal of practicing metta is to help you reverse your programming so you can open your heart rather than close it.

The practice of metta involves four steps. First you start by sending loving-kindness to a family member or dear friend. Next, you send loving-kindness to an acquaintance or someone you are neutral about. Then you send loving-kindness to yourself. The final step is to send loving-kindness to someone you dislike or feel resentful toward. (You may want to start with someone you have a mild aversion to, working your way up to those you have the most dislike for.)

Think of someone who fills each of the categories, and let's begin.

STEP 1: A FAMILY MEMBER OR DEAR FRIEND
Repeat this statement three times:

> I send loving-kindness to _____. My wish is that this person experiences only love and happiness in his/her life.

Close your eyes, and for the next two or three minutes meditate with the intention that the person named receives love and happiness. Visualize them receiving and experiencing these good things, and be as specific in your visualizations as you can.

Step 2: An Acquaintance or Someone You Have Neutral Feelings For

Embody this same sense of loving-kindness toward someone you feel neutral about. Practice cultivating the same amount of loving-kindness that you felt in the first practice.

> I send loving-kindness to _____. My wish is that this person experiences only love and happiness in his/her life.

Repeat this statement three times, then close your eyes, and for the next two or three minutes meditate with the intention that the person named receives love and happiness. Visualize them receiving and experiencing these good things, and be as specific in your visualizations as you can.

Step 3: Yourself

This one can often be as hard as Step 4, and it creates a wonderful practice to set aside any judgments you have about yourself, if even for just a few minutes.

> I send loving-kindness to myself. My wish is that I experience only love and happiness in my life.

Repeat the above statement three times, then close your eyes, and for the next two or three minutes meditate with the intention that you receive abundant love and happiness in your life. Visualize yourself receiving and experiencing these good things, and be as specific in your visualizations as you can.

Step 4: Someone You Dislike

Finally, embody loving-kindness toward someone you dislike. I suggest starting with a person you have a mild aversion to, and moving on to the more difficult resentments as you become more experienced with this practice. This is usually the most difficult part of the metta practice, but it is also the most liberating.

> I send loving-kindness to _____. My wish is that this person experiences only love and happiness in his/her life.

Repeat the above statement three times, then close your eyes, and for the next two or three minutes meditate with the intention that the person named above receives love and happiness. Visualize them receiving and experiencing these good things, and be as specific in your visualizations as you can.

Do this practice over and over again. If you get stuck, go back a step and anchor the feeling of loving-kindness in your heart again. You are rewiring yourself from the inside out, and doing so involves actually practicing loving-kindness via this exercise, not just thinking about it as a concept.

Lesson

7

7.4 Ho'oponopono Practice

Ho'oponopono is an ancient Hawaiian practice similar to metta, but the focus is on forgiveness rather than loving-kindness. This ritual has brought about incredible change in those who have undertaken it.

To begin, think of someone you have had a conflict with. This can be past or present, a loud and bitter conflict, or a quiet and unspoken feud. Hold a vision of this person in your mind and make the following statements internally or out loud (I recommend out loud!).

I love you.

I'm sorry.

Please forgive me.

Thank you.

Repeat the above exercise with the same person in mind every day for five days, and see how you feel. I can't say enough good things about this ancient practice. Many who have undertaken it have experienced a dramatic shift in their relationship with the other party within days of implementation. Try it for yourself and experience the gifts. If you want to learn more about ho'oponopono, Joe Vitale's book *Zero Limits* is an excellent resource.

7.5 Set Heart Boundaries

Some of us have an old belief system that equates saying no with being unloving; but oftentimes saying no is exactly what love asks of us. This exercise is designed to help clear up the misperception that if you love someone you should say yes to him or her all the time. This includes yourself, too—sometimes you must give yourself a loving no as well.

Here are a few examples of what it looks like to set loving boundaries:

My friend is frustrated with me because I have some unexpected free time and I choose to work on a project instead of having lunch with her. She shares that she's upset and she wants to see me. I feel myself think,

"Well, it is just lunch, and I do want to see her. I can make it happen." But first I open my heart and breathe. And from a loving place within, I see that what will serve me best is to continue with my project. Staying open to my truth, and also to her truth that she is upset and feels rejected by me in this moment, I let her know that I can't do lunch, but I could meet her for tea the next morning or we can set up another lunch date when I return from my travels. I don't try to change her feelings of disappointment or justify my decision; I simply share my truth and give some open-hearted options.

My teenage daughter wants to go to a particular friend's house and spend the night, but last time she went to this friend's house the parents let them have a party (including the use of alcohol and drugs). Things got out of hand, and the police were called. My daughter promises me that this time will be different and offers many assurances, but my intuitive sense and past experience tell me that she shouldn't be allowed to go. I decide to tell her that she can't go over there tonight, but that the friend is welcome at our house.

My mouth wants that piece of chocolate. But I open my heart and say no to myself because I am sick and know sugar will slow down my recovery.

Lesson

7

A great new opportunity shows up at work. I open my heart and choose to say no to the opportunity because I don't want to overwhelm myself. I recognize that I am involved with a lot right now, and I need to save time for rest and relaxation.

Now it's your turn. Consider how you've approached boundaries in the past, and how you'd like to approach them in the future.

What loving boundaries have you set for others recently?

_____

_____

_____

_____

_____

What loving boundaries have you set for yourself?

_____

_____

_____

_____

_____

What loving boundaries would you like to set for others in the future? Can you take action on any of these today, or this week?

_____

_____

_____

_____

_____

*Open
Your
Heart*

What loving boundaries would you like to set for yourself in the future? Can you take action on any of these today, or this week?

_____

_____

_____

_____

_____

_____

_____

Sometimes there are things you really don't want to do, but you also recognize that in the long run it will be beneficial, or it is important to you. When these situations arise and you take action that a part of you doesn't want to perform, instead of acting from resentment or resistance, feel your love or gratitude for the relationships you are nourishing with your action, and practice loving what is.

Next time you feel an intuitive nudge to question whether or not you should say yes or no to something, practice the following steps:

1. Take a deep breath, and visualize it going deep into your heart.

2. Call the feeling of love into your heart and being.

3. Listen to what will serve you best from a place of self-love.

7.6 Heart-Opening Practice

Sometimes touch can help us unlock our hidden agreements. In this exercise, you're going to massage out with love all the old agreements blocking your heart.

Begin by massaging your breasts, feeling them as an extension of your heart. Feel the muscles around your chest, and bring healing touch to any armoring. Massage your arms and hands, and imagine opening up your hands so more energy can pour down into everything you touch. Massage out with love all the old agreements that keep your heart chakra closed. You may want to speak out loud what you are releasing. Then use your gentle touch to massage in healing and aliveness.

Now consciously practice standing up straight, breasts out, heart open, as you interact in the world. Notice when you want to contract or slouch. Notice the difference in your being energetically when you collapse your chest versus when you consciously open it.

7.7 Discover What Feeds Your Heart

When you are making a decision, ask yourself, does this nourish my heart? What shift do I need to make so my heart feels fed? Get beyond your stories of what you want and listen to your heart, not your mind! You will need to get quiet and listen in a new way. There may still be fear and difficult choices, but your heart's voice will ring sweetly.

What does your heart want with respect to the following:

- Your relationship with your family
- Your intimate relationships
- Your career

Additional Gifts

- An open heart is grounded in self-compassion and rooted in respect.

- Let your heart soar by honoring its strength and resiliency.

- Love your flaws, your fears, and your struggles. Let nothing on the inside be outside of your acceptance.

- You don't have to agree with others' behaviors or beliefs to continue to hold loving-kindness.

Lesson
7

Lesson 8

Speak Your Truth

From
Warrior Goddess Training

When you do not speak your truth and either hold it inside or placate others, you often end up carrying resentment. You get mad at yourself for not speaking your mind or mad at others for not understanding how you really feel (forgetting that you never told them how you feel!). In organizations and family systems, this creates distrust, gossip, and fear, and what is commonly referred to as "drama." When resentment builds up, we sometimes explode in a venting of emotions and judgment in an unconscious or punishing manner. When this occurs, you are not speaking from a place of love, but rather from your wounds and hurt, often not realizing your part in the situation, which was that you did not communicate how you really felt in the first place. Intimate relationships then become hollow and dissatisfying, and your own trust of self is diminished each time you do not speak what you really mean.

To find and maintain balance, we must evaluate and unweave any old agreements that we have around verbal communication. Remember that your destination is to experience open-hearted, fluid communication and vibrant expression, using your inner knowing as a guide. As coach and author Martha Beck says, "No matter how difficult and painful it may be, nothing sounds as good to the soul as the truth."

Lesson

8

I still sometimes struggle to speak my truth with the people closest to me. Some days I don't want to hurt them, or rock the boat, or be vulnerable. I want them to read my mind or just change their behavior on their own. My old agreements and stories can kick in, closing down my voice even when I want to speak. When this happens, I've learned to not berate myself, but instead to realize that I need extra inner support at these times of fear to break through the old patterns and share my inner world.

When you don't speak your truth from your heart, you create a space for resentment or frustration to take root. Conversely, speaking your truth can create bridges in relationships, deepening the intimacy you have with yourself and others.

Unfortunately, as women, we often learn that communication should always be harmonious or pleasant. But sometimes the best, most transformative conversations are the difficult ones.

Your truth is precious. You may choose not to share it with everyone under all circumstances, and that's understandable. But there is one person to whom you must always speak your truth: yourself.

The purpose of this lesson is to spot and release old beliefs around communication with yourself and others, and to create a new plan for speaking your truth going forward.

Exercises

8.1 Find Your Truth

To learn more about your own truth in communicating, circle True or False next to the statements in the chart that follows. In addition, write down anything else you believe about how you should communicate in the world. Read the list over and notice which agreements are about getting a desired result or reaction from the person you are talking to, and which stem from your authentic expression.

Growing up, I was taught or believed:

Children and/or girls should be seen and not heard.	True/False
It is better to lie to someone if you think the truth will hurt him/her.	True/False
Women who "speak their mind" are bossy.	True/False
Women should support whatever their partner prefers.	True/False
Women should put the needs of others ahead of their own.	True/False
Women should be demure and quiet.	True/False
Girls shouldn't like loud things.	True/False
It is better to not say anything than to upset others.	True/False

Once you've finished, review your answers. Which agreements are about getting a desired result or reaction from the person you are talking to? Do any of these agreements stem from your authentic expression?

8.2 Write It Out

We know now that looking deeply into our unconscious beliefs is crucial. Is it okay for you to say no? Is it okay for you to make boundaries? Is it okay for you to say things others may not want to hear? Can you speak without taking responsibility for others' reactions? And can you do all of these things with your heart wide open?

In the space that follows or your notebook, write out the affirmative answer to the questions above. Begin each sentence with "I am free to . . ." For example:

- I am free to say no.
- I am free to set boundaries.
- I am free to say things others might not want to hear.
- I am free to speak without taking responsibility for others' reactions to my words.
- I am free to speak with my heart wide open.

Now it's your turn. Write the above, or something similar, here:

Notice how you feel after writing out your affirmative statements. Do this exercise every morning until you feel the truth of these ideas at your innermost core; then watch as you manifest that truth in the world.

8.3 Vocalize Your Truth

Change rarely occurs if we continue to do the same things and simply hope for different results. The purpose of this exercise is to free your voice by using it in new and unexpected ways. The following suggestions may seem odd at first, but they will help you create different ways to express yourself through your voice this week. Here are some ideas:

- Sing animatedly to songs on the radio.
- Pick three animals and mimic their sounds aloud (try a monkey, a bird, and a lioness to start).
- Make strange noises as you drive to work.
- Have animated conversations with yourself in the mirror.
- Hum and make the *om* sound at different tones and volumes.
- Go to a river or stream and get close; let your voice mirror the sound of the water.

As you do these, notice what agreements and judgments about your voice show up. How does being vocal make you feel? Remember, all of these can be done in private, so there's no need to feel self-conscious.

8.4 Stop Saying Yes When You Mean No

The fastest way to create discomfort and resentment in your life is to say yes when you mean no. If someone asks you to do something and you say yes out of a feeling of obligation, or because you don't want to hurt the other person's feelings, then you are not speaking your truth. Being your true, authentic, Warrior Goddess self means saying no from a place of love rather than saying yes from a place of fear.

In the space below, list any situations in the recent past when you have said yes when you really meant no.

Here are some examples:

- Someone invited me to a dinner party and I went even though I didn't want to.
- I loaned money to a friend again even though she hasn't paid back the last loan.
- My boss asked me to take another project at work and I said yes even though I'll have to stay late to do it.

_____

_____

_____

_____

_____

_____

_____

Speak
Your
Truth

Now, write how you would like to respond the next time this situation arises.

Here are some examples:

- I'll say thank you for inviting me, but tonight is my night to catch up on home projects.

- I understand you need more money, but I can't loan you any more until the last loan is paid back.

- I appreciate that you came to me with this new project. I have time to work on it today only if I stop working on my other project and we extend the deadline. Or I can start it next week. Which do you prefer?

8.5 Vent, Advice, Share

My friend and I play a simple game that helps us to stay present. It's helpful because it creates a setting where both people know the goal is to have explicitly clear and open conversation.

Start by stating your intention—Vent, Advice, or Share—so your partner knows what's coming next.

- Vent: If one of us needs to vent and express our frustration after a hard day, we say, "Vent!" One person takes five minutes to vent as fully and dramatically as possible, and once those five minutes are up we stop and move on.

- Advice: If we want advice about the situation we are about to share, we say, "Advice!" so that the other person knows to get her creative brain in gear.

- Share: If we say, "Share!" that means, "I'm really excited about something—cheerlead and celebrate with me!"

As with most games, it takes two willing participants. So after you say vent, advice, or share, the other person can say, "Give it to me!" or he or she can also say, "Not now!" which means, "I don't have the space for communicating right now."

Is there someone in your life who would be a helpful partner in this game?

8.6 Unhealthy Communication
As I wrote in *Warrior Goddess Training,*

> Speaking your truth does not mean you always say everything you are thinking . . . Being a Warrior Goddess requires discernment. We must be careful not to use the practice of speaking our truth as an excuse to be cruel or hurtful. Simply put, the spirit of this practice means you are willing to delve deeper into your own truth and your own inner guidance, and you are willing to speak this truth even in situations where your listener may be uncomfortable with what you have to say.

Even though we may have trouble speaking our truth, it doesn't mean we're not communicating. When we get upset and don't speak our truth clearly, we sometimes communicate in one of two unhealthy manners: passive aggressive behavior or using words as weapons.

PASSIVE AGGRESSIVE BEHAVIOR
Passive aggressive communication occurs when you don't express how you really feel, but instead pretend to be okay with a situation while still attempting to manipulate it to reach the outcome you desire. Communicating in this manner is the opposite of speaking your truth, and it can cause resentment and hurt feelings in relationships.

For example, if your partner says or does something you don't like and then asks if you are okay with it, a passive aggressive response would be, "That's fine, if it's what you want." In reality, you weren't fine with it at all, and you now have not expressed your truth and created an internal resentment. You may then follow up by acting in a way that is contrary to what you stated, or subverts what you just agreed to. Here's how this might play out:

Partner: "I'd like to go out with some friends from the office tonight. Are you okay with that? And could we make dinner together a little earlier so I can do so?"

You're disappointed, but instead you say, "That's fine, if it's what you want to do."

Partner: "Are you sure? Because I can do it another night."

You: "No, go ahead . . . Do what you want." Then you slow down on your part of dinner in an attempt to subvert your partner's plans.

Conversely, if you were to speak your truth in the situation without any passive aggressive speech, you might say, "I'm disappointed. I really wanted to spend time with you tonight," and then you could search inside yourself and decide if you can support your partner's decision, try and find an alternative solution, or accept his or her decision while noting your disagreement.

This example is a relatively minor situation, but the goal is to bring this level of honesty and open-mindedness to all of your communication.

USING WORDS AS WEAPONS

Words can be weapons when our intent is to cause pain in another person with our speech. As a Warrior Goddess, you want to strive to speak your truth in a way that is clear but that doesn't add unnecessary insult or accusations. For example, I have a friend who shares joint custody of her daughter with her ex-husband, and he often doesn't fulfill their agreement when it comes to spending time with her. Prior to reading *Warrior Goddess Training*, when he would miss a pickup time she would call and say something like this: "You missed another pickup time for your daughter. You are such a lousy father. I hope you realize the damage you are doing to our little girl. I can't believe I was ever married to you."

After reading *Warrior Goddess Training*, her conversation went more like this: "You missed another pickup time for your daughter. This makes her sad, because she wants to see you; if you can't pick her up when you are scheduled to do so, I'll need you and I to come to another agreement on visitation."

And while changing her communication may or may not affect a change in the behavior, my friend reports that she feels much better about the way in which she is now communicating with her ex-husband, and is creating less negative energy in the process.

Conversely, passive aggressive communication can also cause resentment and hurt feelings in relationships. When we feel injured, many of us have reverted to passive aggressiveness or using words as weapons, and sometimes both. Becoming aware of when and why we communicate in these unhealthy ways is the first step in correcting the behavior.

Can you think of a time when you have made passive aggressive statements or used words as weapons? Write the instances out below or in your notebook.

_____

_____

_____

_____

_____

Now it's time for a redo. In your mind's eye, put yourself back in that situation. What could you have said instead? How could you have communicated your heart's truth in a way that was clear and also filled with the spirit of love? Remember, this doesn't mean that the other person may not feel saddened or otherwise upset by what you have to say, but the point is you are being conscious of speaking from a place of love rather than fear, knowing that the other person's reaction is beyond your control. Write this alternative communication down below. This is great practice for the next time you are in a similar situation.

_____

_____

_____

_____

Lesson
8

8.7 The Much-Needed Conversation

Is there a conversation that you need to have with someone but have been afraid to initiate? Can you set a goal and make a plan to do this within the next thirty days? What are the main points you want to make, and why? How do you feel about the situation? Write them out below or in your notebook.

_____

_____

_____

_____

_____

_____

Remember, your plan is to speak with your heart wide open, and come from a place of love rather than fear. Try and avoid statements of judgment regarding the other person's behavior, and stick to the facts and what is really in your heart.

After you've made your plan, let it sit for a day or two, and then revisit it. Feel free to edit and adjust it after you've had time to reflect.

Once you are at peace with what's on the page, use these talking points as a guide to have that conversation. Remember, your purpose is to speak your truth. How the other person interprets the information is up to them.

Additional Gifts

- Start with a beginner's mind as you learn to communicate from your deepest truth.
- If you find yourself uncomfortable with finding the words to express yourself, that often means you are growing past your old communication habits.
- Intimacy comes from sharing your observations, thoughts, feelings, and needs with yourself first, and then with those closest to you. Embrace your vulnerabilities.
- No matter how difficult the conversation, keep your heart open—especially toward yourself.

Lesson 9

Embody Your Wisdom

From

Warrior Goddess Training

Our intuition is proof that there is more to life than what can be weighed, measured, or otherwise quantified in a lab. The laws of science cannot explain intuition, yet we all know it's real based on personal experience. By definition, intuition is from the realm of the spiritual.

Closely related to intuition is the concept of wisdom. This is not the type of wisdom that can be gained from reading a book; rather, it is more like a deep sense of knowing, a feeling that comes from your heart. When you think and act from this seat of wisdom, you move along the path of life, tapping into the strength to deal with whatever may come your way.

Lesson
9

In the last lesson you learned to use your voice to express yourself. In this lesson, the focus is on learning to listen to your innermost self, which speaks to you through the silent voices of wisdom and intuition.

Growing up, most of us were taught to ignore or diminish our intuitive voice, and listen to or validate the critical and fearful voices in our mind instead. Warrior Goddess Training is about recognizing which voices are from our internal judge or victim, and which are from our wisdom or intuition. For most of us, this means we are learning how to listen to ourselves in a new way. When you start to listen with every cell of your body rather than just your mind, your world begins to change. You begin to live from the inspirational heart instead of the critical mind.

We all have the ability to tap into the wealth of our intuition and the abundance of our wisdom. This quality of deep listening is found in but not limited to shamans, psychics, healers, and elders. No matter what your age or experience, you too have a direct line to intuition and wisdom. It is not without, but within.

Some of us knew this language as a child, but it was soon drowned out by the louder voices of the outer world. As kids we are rarely taught to get quiet, breathe, and listen before we take action, or to follow our inner promptings and knowings. We are taught how to pay attention to the teacher, the minister, our

Embody Your Wisdom

parents, and to always do what they say, even when our inner knowing is waving red flags.

The portal to access your intuitive wisdom is silence. Learn to be still, and let the loud critical voices of your mind wash through you until you can see the clear waters of your intuition. Learn to love silence, and feel the winds of wisdom clear any internal fog and bring clarity. Learn to slow down, and let the fire of the truth burn away any unwanted brush, revealing the peace that is always within you.

Exercises

9.1 Listen to Your Inner Silence

This brief meditation can help you find the silence within.

Sit comfortably in a room alone and turn off the TV, radio, etc., and set the timer on your phone for between two and ten minutes. If you are new at meditation, I suggest setting the timer to two minutes and increasing the time as you get more comfortable with meditation.

Once the timer is set, close your eyes and go inside. Focus on finding the silence in your mind, which exists in the space between thoughts. As you sit still, thoughts will continue to arise, and that's fine. Don't try to force or stop them. Imagine they are clouds passing through the clear blue sky of your awareness. Just notice the silent space in between or behind this mental flow.

Finding this silence is not something you want to try and force, and please don't judge yourself if it seems difficult to find that silence at first. Instead, just remind yourself that it is there, and sit quietly and bring your focus inward. Experience the power of the present moment. Thoughts come and go, but there is an ever-present silence behind and in between them.

Can you find that still space?

9.2 Do the Opposite

In Exercise 8.3, Vocalize Your Truth, we tried shaking things up by making some silly or unusual sounds. And in Exercise 6.5, Experimenting Beyond Strategies, we practiced the Toltec art of "not doing." Here, we're going to continue building on this idea of breaking up habits by changing your daily routine in new and unexpected ways, as this creates a space for further changes to occur. Try any of the following scenarios for a few days:

- Brush your teeth with the opposite hand.
- Drink your coffee or morning beverage with the opposite hand.
- Drive a new way to work (or school, or the grocery store, or a friend's house).
- Order something completely different for lunch/dinner than you feel like having.

You get the idea. Now, you choose a couple things to do that break a simple routine.

You can create the space for wisdom to arise by doing the opposite of what is most familiar to your mind. In doing so, you are beginning to create an environment that is conducive to change on a larger level. If you usually go immediately to your knowledge to make decisions or to figure things out, slow down, get quiet, and ask your intuition to speak. If you always call someone else to get answers to issues or problems, stop and first open to your own wisdom. If you ignore your intuition in favor of what you think you are supposed to be doing or feeling, turn toward the mystery and ask for the wisdom of the unknown to guide you.

You may not feel like this reconnection to your intuition and wisdom is working at first. But stay the course, even when it feels like nothing is happening. As you unwind the old pattern of putting all your faith in your mind or in the people outside of you, you will start, bit by bit, to bring your natural faith back into your own inner knowing. Slow down. Be patient. Listen, listen, listen.

9.3 Intuition Talk

The purpose of this exercise is to consciously develop your communication with your intuition. Create a quiet space and have a pen and paper nearby.

Imagine that you are having tea with your intuition. Say hello to her, and thank her for meeting with you. Then, ask your intuition how you can better listen to her, and if she has any information for you at this time. Write your intuition's answers down. Next, ask any specific questions you have for your intuition.

For some, just visualizing that you are talking to your intuition will help you get more insights. For others, it might be necessary to write down your questions first and let your intuition answer through your writing. Whatever your method, keep opening up the channel of communication between yourself and your intuition until the dialogue becomes seamless.

9.4 Intuition Visualization

Create a quiet space to practice this next visualization. Sit comfortably in a chair or on the floor, and ground yourself by sinking your roots deep into the earth. Call up the earth's energy into your body using your imagination and your breath. As you breathe the energy up through your roots, imagine you are listening to the ancient silence of the rocks buried deep in the earth. Feel the wisdom of the ancestors in the soil. Rest into the stillness of earth, and let her wisdom soak through your roots and into your bones.

Now breathe into your full body, and listen to the silence within your bones. Feel the ancient wisdom of your DNA. Rest into the stillness of your being, and let your cellular wisdom unfold like a flower in sunlight.

Imagine you can open the top of your head and send branches into the sky. Imagine your branches reaching out and touching the vastness of space, the wisdom of the stars, the mysteries of the Universe. Breathe the sunlight and moonlight and starlight down into your body, asking the light of these radiant beings to help awaken your innate wisdom.

Know yourself as the daughter of Mother Earth and Father Sun. Feel their immense love and faith in you. Breathe it in. Let this connection to your spiritual parents of earth and sky dissolve your old human programming and fill you with peace, grace, and the wisdom of the Universe.[3]

9.5 Identify Your Filters

Sometimes your initial intuitive sense is clear, but then you filter the message through your opinions and experiences, and the desires and fears of the mind take over. As a result, the original truth of your intuition is clouded, obscured. What are some of your personal filters that may cloud your intuition? Here is a way to help identify them.

---

3 Please visit www.warriorgoddessaudio.com to download a free extended audio version of this exercise.

Ask yourself the following questions, and write down your responses in the space provided or in your notebook:

- What did I learn from my parents about intuition?
- What did I learn from my church/temple/school about spirit and inner wisdom?
- Is there any way I am afraid of my intuition?
- What does it mean to be a spiritual person?
- Is there any way I give my intuitive abilities over to someone else?

_____

_____

_____

_____

_____

_____

_____

9.6 Watch the Outcome

"Watch the outcome" works like this: When you have what you believe to be an intuitive feeling or response, take a moment to jot it down. Think of a time when you had an intuitive feeling, and answer the questions in the space that follows:

- What was your flash of intuition?
- Where were you and what were you doing when you experienced it?
- Where did you sense the intuition in your body?

- Did you hear a voice? What did it sound like?
- How did you feel emotionally?

_____

_____

_____

_____

_____

_____

_____

Track all the different aspects of what you perceive to be your intuition. The next time you have what you feel is an intuitive message, make a conscious decision to follow it or not follow it. With the benefit of hindsight, ask yourself, was that message from your intuition or your mind? How did things unfold? By writing things down and then watching the outcome, you will begin to recognize where you were clear and where you were off target. Over time, you will find that you get much better in your ability to identify which feelings are likely intuitive and which ones are not (but are coming from your core strategies).

Here are a few examples of watching the outcome and tracking your intuition versus your mind's habits:

Date: 6/8/14

Feeling/thought: I feel certain that I'm making the wrong choice about my career.

Action: I sat in meditation, then made a list of pros and cons.

Details: It took a long time to quiet the internal fear and open myself to listening for what is true. I kept breathing and letting go until I felt more centered and at peace. As I made my lists, I noticed that each time I listed a possible negative outcome I felt scared, and each time I listed a possible positive outcome I felt excited. I realized I woke up "reading" the fear list to myself over and over again.

Result: I talked to the part of myself that is scared and let it know everything is going to be okay. Then I started focusing on where I wanted to go rather than what might go wrong.

What I learned: Strong emotions do not mean I am making a wrong choice. Sometimes I just need to self-soothe when I am going through a big change.

New action: Always get quiet first and soothe myself before I act on a fear.

Date: 1/9/15

Feeling/thought: I need to call my friend right away.

Action: I almost disregarded this impulse because I had just talked to my friend a few days earlier. But I picked up the phone and left a message, then checked her Facebook page.

Details: Her Facebook post said she was at the emergency room with her mother, who had fallen and broken her hip.

Result: I called my friend's husband, and he asked me to pick up their kids. I was able to rearrange my schedule to pick up the kids, drop them off at home, and then meet my friend at the hospital and bring her some food.

What I learned: An intuitive sign can come at any moment.

New action: I should follow up on my inner nudges, even if they don't seem logical or necessary.

When you are watching the outcome, it is important to not judge yourself. Remember, you are learning. Be curious and patient about the subtle differences between an intuitive knowing and a mind story. As you can tease apart the threads of old habits and fears and reweave your life from the stronger weaving of inner knowing, you will open to the fountain of sacred wisdom that flows within you.

Now it's your turn. Here is space to write down three examples of your own witnessing:

Date: _____

Feeling/thought: _____

_____

_____

_____

_____

Action: _____

_____

Embody Your Wisdom

_____

_____

_____

_____

Details: _____

_____

_____

_____

_____

Result: _____

_____

_____

_____

_____

What I learned: _____

_____

_____

_____

_____

_____

Lesson
9

New action (if applicable): _____

_____

_____

_____

_____

_____

❖❖❖

Date: _____

Feeling/thought: _____

_____

_____

_____

_____

Action: _____

_____

_____

_____

_____

Details: _____

Embody
Your
Wisdom

— 139 —

_____

_____

_____

_____

Result: _____

_____

_____

_____

_____

What I learned: _____

_____

_____

_____

_____

Lesson
_9_

New action (if applicable): _____

_____

_____

_____

_____

❖❖❖

Date: _____

Feeling/thought: _____

_____

_____

_____

_____

_____

Action: _____

_____

_____

_____

_____

Details: _____

Embody
Your
Wisdom

_____

_____

_____

_____

Result: _____

_____

_____

_____

_____

What I learned: _____

_____

_____

_____

_____

New action (if applicable): _____

_____

_____

_____

_____

Lesson
9

9.7 Deepen Your Silence

Now that you are firmly planted on the Warrior Goddess path, it's time to raise your commitment to your spiritual practices. The following exercises will help you be more in touch with your intuition and wisdom. As you try each activity, record your specific experience either here or in your notebook.

1. Once a week, take one hour to be in silence.

My experience: _____

_____

_____

_____

_____

2. Practice partial silence at a party or at work. Limit your speaking to only what is necessary. Fill the spaces between with love or a specific intent.

My experience: _____

_____

_____

_____

_____

3. Several times a day, stop multitasking. When you are eating, just eat. When you are talking on the phone, just talk.

My experience: _____

_____

_____

_____

_____

_____

4. Create more spaciousness in each moment through your conscious breath and intent. Even when you are really busy, you can slow yourself down and feel into the silence between seconds. Notice that you are breathing. Watch the gap that occurs between the in-breath and the out-breath.

My experience: _____

_____

_____

_____

_____

5. Plan a time for an extended silence, perhaps several hours or even a day or two. Get clear on what you will need to do to make this happen. Ask for support. Create guidelines for yourself.

My experience: _____

_____

_____

_____

_____

_____

Lesson
9

6. If you usually are silent in the world, do just the opposite! Run experiments to talk more and express yourself. Look at what will challenge you the most.

My experience: _____

_____

_____

_____

_____

Additional Gifts

- When you become open to listening to your inner voice, you realize that your intuition is always guiding you.

- Become intimate with your unique style of inner perception. Do you gather information through visual pictures or symbols, your body and feeling, an inner voice, or an unexplainable knowing?

- In the space between the words and the gaps between thoughts rests the wide-open vastness of silent knowledge.

Embody
Your
Wisdom

Lesson 10

Choose Your Path

From
Warrior Goddess Training

A role is a script written long before you were born. A role defines how you should act, how you should respond, and what you should believe. We often take on a role without recognizing it is a role, and then suddenly we find ourselves acting in ways we don't like or understand. When we identify with a role, we believe it is who we are, not just a part we are playing.

This is the truth: You are not any of these identities; they are simply the roles, or masks, that you have taken on. No matter how much you love or hate the role, or how firm the mask is, the role is not the totality of you. You are the changeless force beneath the masks, the divine presence that makes the mask possible. Knowing this is the wisdom of the Warrior Goddess.

Lesson
10

As a Warrior Goddess, you are fluid like water, you illuminate like fire, you are strong like earth, and you are powerful like the wind. You are a goddess of life, and a warrior of the heart.

By going deeper with each of the Warrior Goddess lessons, you'll find that you have more energy, awareness, and focus in your life. You'll also start to notice that the old roles no longer fit who you are becoming, and you will begin to create an external world that authentically matches who you are on the inside.

You can now consciously choose which paths you want to take in life, as well as the roles you want to play on your journey.

Understanding that you are not any predetermined roles frees you to choose what role you do want to play. And it is play, a choice to take on a particular role, embody it fully, and then let it go. Because you are the water, the fire, the earth, and the wind, and no role can contain your vastness. And yet it is super fun to choose which role you want to experience for today, knowing you can change it tomorrow if you choose.

Exercises

10.1 Infinity Visualization

Create a quiet space for this next visualization. The purpose of this exercise is to remind you that you can be anything you want to be; there are an infinite number of choices in front of you.

To begin, imagine your roots going deep into the earth. Take a deep breath, and visualize that you are drawing up the earth energy into your heart. Hold your breath and let your heart expand.

When you are ready to exhale, breathe all the way out through the top of your head and out your branches into the sky. Hold your breath on the exhale.

Then inhale deeply, bringing the energy from the sky down into your heart. Hold your breath, and let earth and sky mix in your heart.

Then exhale from heart to earth, and hold the breath.

Inhale, pulling earth energy up into your heart. Hold your breath.

Exhale from heart to sky, and hold the breath.

Inhale from sky to heart, and hold the breath.

Then exhale from heart to earth.

Use this simple breathing technique to release your thoughts and connect to your heart. When you feel grounded and expanded, imagine that you are creating an infinity loop that dives into the earth and up into the sky, and crosses at your heart. Breathe into your heart and let the energy move in this beautiful infinity sign.[4]

10.2 Identify Your Roles

In this exercise, you're going to define your roles and come up with a plan to change or maintain each one. First, think about the roles you currently have, and list them in your notebook. Here are some places to start:

- At work or at school
- In your family

---

4   Please visit www.warriorgoddessaudio.com to download a free extended audio version of this exercise.

- In your intimate relationships
- With your friends
- With your neighbors

Here's one example of a role: perfect wife. The process of writing this down can help you better understand that the role you are playing is just that—a role. It's not you.

Next, describe how you play each role. Continuing the example from above, you might say something like this:

> It started with trying to be who I thought my spouse wanted me to be when we got married a couple of years ago. I try to be June Cleaver even when he doesn't want me to. It's just a fantasy in my head of what I should be capable of. Even though I am working full-time, I try to cook every meal, do the laundry, and keep the house spotless. I spend all my time at home and don't do anything for myself.

Third, go down your list and consider which roles are still serving you, and which aren't. Which ones are you attached to? Those probably need to go. Mark off with a checkmark or star the roles that are no longer serving you.

Finally, decide what action you want to take regarding each role. For example, you might say,

> I want to enjoy my spouse and our home rather than trying to make everything perfect. I'm going to let him share responsibility for cleaning and cooking, and let go of my crazy standards in exchange for more peace.

There are no right or wrong answers. The point of the exercise is to recognize the roles and release any that are no longer serving you.

Here are a couple more examples:

Role: Healer

Description: I am a massage therapist who takes my role of healing people very seriously. But it has gotten out of control, as I keep giving away free or hugely discounted sessions to whomever asks. Even though I'm working full-time I can't make enough money to pay my bills. I feel like I'm bad if I want to take care of myself.

Action: I'm ready to bring my healing to myself. Next month I am going to raise my prices to the going rate, and only do one free session a week. I'm also going to follow up with my inspiration to do massage at corporations. I release holding the role of healer in the places it is hurting me so I can bring my gifts forward from inspiration rather than obligation.

Role: Mother

Description: Even though I don't have kids, at work I have taken on the role of being everyone's mother. I stay late to clean other people's messes, overly nurture the team even when I don't agree with them, and am always willing to take on more work if someone needs help, even when I can't get my own work done. I'm getting burnt out and resentful.

Action: I'm going to go back to my job description and remind myself about my scope of work. Then I'm going to start treating everyone as a capable adult instead of like a child. I'm willing to give up the illusion of being able to handle everything and start asking for help.

This is the truth: you are not any of these identities; they are simply the roles, or masks, that you have taken on. No matter how much you love or hate the role, or how firm the mask is, the role is not the totality of you. You are the changeless force beneath the masks, the divine presence that makes the mask possible. Knowing this is the wisdom of the Warrior Goddess.

As you transition out of a role that is familiar, it can be uncomfortable, scary, and awkward as you stabilize a new way of being. It can also be fun, too, as you learn to shed the old and try new things. Stay steady with your new actions, and correct your course when you slip back into the old role. Keep reminding yourself why you are releasing the role, so you can be making choices from the fullness of this "I choose to" present moment rather than from the heaviness of an "I have to" past.

As you go beneath these different roles to the core of you, find the essence that has remained stable through each identity. Writing out the answers to the following questions will help you find this essence.

- Can you find the seed of your light beneath the roles? What does that feel like?
- Go back to who you were before you were attached to any roles, when you were a small child. What do you notice?
- Can you remember fully experiencing something without thought, reflection, or judgment? These are the moments when there is no role, no narrator of who you should be, no regard for what others think. These are the moments of you being you, fully.

10.3 The Power of Myth

To become more flexible in your roles, you can explore what I call your big myth and your little myth. Your big myth is the story you create of why you are here; your little myth is a role you are choosing to embody in the short term.

Humans have been telling stories since the beginning of civilization. They help us explain or otherwise make sense of the world around us. We are constantly writing myths about ourselves and others, often without realizing it, and one of the arts of the Warrior Goddess is her willingness to create her own mythology. Claiming your Warrior Goddess path means *choosing* what myth you want to play with, a myth that nourishes you and keeps you energized.

In this section, we will experiment with two types of myths: the big myth, which gives you sacred context, and the little myth, which gives you focus.

YOUR BIG MYTH

Your big myth is the big picture for how and why your unique, precious Warrior Goddess light arrived on the planet.

Dreaming your big myth is first and foremost about outrageous, fabulous, expansive imagination. Go big. Be the heroine of your own story. Have a great support team. Give yourself superpowers.

The possibilities are endless:

- I am an angel finding her wings again.
- I am a warrior of light, sent by my tribe to explore earth.
- I am a messenger of faith here to share my heart and scatter seeds of love everywhere I go.

- I bring peace and connection from the very center of the Universe.

Pick a big myth that makes you glow. Forget sensible or practical or real. Make it big, magic medicine that you incarnated with. Choose your big myth consciously, but hold it lightly; do not get attached! It is a robe to wear, not your true self. Your essence cannot be defined or limited.

My bigger myth is that I am a daughter of the Goddess. My Goddess Mother loves me fiercely and always supports and holds me energetically. I am in service to her and my brothers and sisters, from minerals to plants to people. When I feel this myth my whole body relaxes, and I feel inspired, loved, and loving. I feel happy and confident.

Write a few examples of what your bigger myth is in the space below or in your notebook:

_____

_____

_____

_____

_____

_____

Choose Your Path

Holding a big myth allows you to be honest and creative about assessing and cleaning up mistakes. Do angels get punished? Would the Goddess beat you for bouncing your checkbook, or losing your job, or having an affair? Would she say to you, "Well, you made the same mistake again, but go back to sleep. Maybe if you hide from it something will change." No! But from the place of your big myth, you can see what changes you would like to make without beating yourself up.

Your Little Myth

If your big myth is the big picture for how and why you arrived on the planet, your little myth is the window you choose to shine that light through in your day-to-day life.

Your little myth is like a really fabulous outfit. It's a conscious choice of what persona or role you want to explore in your daily life. Dig through the box and find the perfect outfit for what you want to create at this particular time of your life. What energy are you wanting to bring through into the world?

Here are some little myth roles you could try on: artist, healer, student, teacher, lover, mother, friend, employer, employee, coworker.

Write out some examples of your little myth here or in your notebook:

_____

_____

_____

_____

_____

_____

Don't pick just the roles you are most familiar with. The key to using your little myth to support your growth is to not base it on what society or critics or your friends think you should be (or who you believe they want you to be).

Additional questions to consider are,

What little myth would best serve me now? What action do I want to support myself in taking at this time? What window do I want to shine my light through?

_____

_____

_____

_____

_____

What you are going for in a little myth is a framework that reminds you who you want to be. So when you wake up in the morning, you know why you are here (big myth) *and* you know what your focus for the day is (little myth).

Use your little myth as a way to identify, create, and fulfill your current life purpose. Your little myth will change throughout your life, as you may be a student for a while, then a mother, a teacher, or an artist. You can also have more than one little myth at a time. Just make sure that the little myth or myths you choose are where you want to go, not where you have been. Then your little myth will help break old, stagnant roles.

As a Warrior Goddess, you know that both the big and little myths are ultimately just that—myths. The real you is much, much greater than what can be encapsulated in any story, and consciously choosing which myths you want to create rather than accepting the stories that were created for you is what being a Warrior Goddess is all about.

10.4 Help Others Heal

As Warrior Goddess women, we can bring healing back to the planet and the people. We must be brave, open, trusting, and giving. We need to move past old stories of being ladylike or non-threatening or normal and break the chains of our fears to share our gifts fully. The world is waiting with open hands. It is time to stop isolating ourselves. It is time to step up to serve all.

Practicing the lessons of the Warrior Goddess path and healing yourself from the inside out are the best things you can do for the world. As Mahatma Gandhi said, "Be the change you wish to see in the world."

From this place of love and healing, think of ways you can be helpful to those around you. Remember, there is no need to be grandiose in your answers here, as being helpful in little ways are typically some of the most helpful. Here are some ideas:

- Once a month, spend time with an elderly neighbor.
- Offer to babysit a friend's child so she can have some time off.
- Practice seeing the best in everyone.
- Join a volunteer organization.
- Mentor a young person at work.
- Share your gratitude with a woman who has supported you.
- Give a donation to a local organization that supports women. (No amount is too small!)
- Give a donation to a global organization that supports women. (No amount is too large!)

How can you be of service while staying true to yourself?

_____

_____

_____

_____

_____

10.5 Choose Your Path Self-Check

Congratulations! You have reached the final exercise. Hooray for you!!

What Activities Make You Happy?

In a moment, you're going to write a list of all the activities that make you happy. This list may have expanded since you began *Warrior Goddess Training,* because you now have more clarity about what you want from life.

As an example, my list looks like this: I enjoy gardening, writing, teaching, horseback riding, practicing yoga, meditating, hiking, dancing, reading new books, traveling to new and exotic places, cooking, walking on fire (yes, you read that correctly!), being in the company of friends and loved ones on a regular basis, and volunteering. I could keep going, but I think you get the gist.

Now it's your turn: In the space below or in your notebook, make a list of all the things you enjoy doing.

_____

_____

_____

_____

_____

_____

_____

_____

_____

_____

How Many of These Activities Have You Done in the Last Three Months?

Now it's time to examine how you are actually spending your time on a day-to-day basis. Which activities from your list have you done in the last three months?

Compare and Adjust

As you know, *Warrior Goddess Training* isn't about just planning change or thinking about how to change (although those are necessary first steps); it's about *enacting* those changes, and you will know you have claimed your path when your actions in the world match who you are on the inside.

For me, I can say that I have done 80 percent or more of the things on my list in the past ninety days. Yay for me, and I see where I would like to do more of the things that I love!

While there may be times that your ability to do what you love is limited, such as when you or a loved one is sick or you have a big project at work, the important thing is that these time periods should be temporary—because if they're not, that's likely an indicator that more change is necessary.

Remember, if you're not doing as much on your list as you'd like to, please don't use this as fuel to judge yourself for "not being a good Warrior Goddess." The point of this exercise is to lovingly notice where you need to make more adjustments, and support yourself with gentle kindness as you get there.

Choose
Your
Path

Epilogue

From
Warrior Goddess Training

In my dream all women recognize their worth, their wisdom, the healing power of their laughter. We hold hands across nations, across religions, across divisions. And we reach out to invite every child, every man, every single being regardless of gender or belief or experience, to hold hands with us. We weave a web of acceptance, respect, love, and forgiveness. And then we get to work celebrating life, dancing through our fears, and nurturing the sassy spark within each of us.

Be a Warrior Goddess. Keep cleaning, keep living the Warrior Goddess lessons. Commit to You. Align with Life. Purify Your Vessel. Ground Your Being, and Free Your Past. Energize Your Sexuality and Creativity. Claim Your Strength and Ignite Your Will. Open Your Heart. Speak Your Truth. Embody Your Wisdom. Choose Your Path. Repeat.

Epilogue

Keep saying yes to yourself and let the nectar of your yes overflow so others can find their unique, divine yes. Be an inspiration. Be yourself.

The purpose of Warrior Goddess Training is to create an external reality that matches who you authentically are on the inside, and the proof to yourself that you are on the path can be found in your actions. When you find that you aren't honoring who you really are or what you really want, then it's time to course correct with love. The Warrior Goddess path is never-ending, and the beauty is to be found in the journey.

Whether or not we ever meet in physical form, know that my body is your body, my heart is your heart, and my love is your love. We are warriors and goddesses across time and space, supporting each other as we make the internal and external worlds more beautiful in the process. Namaste, dear ones. The Spirit within me salutes the Spirit within you.

Epilogue

Your Questions Answered

Question

Is it normal to feel utter resistance and a desire to NOT do Warrior Goddess Training? I kept resisting the urge to close this book and get rid of it. Maybe I need this more than I think I do!!!!

Answer

First of all, thank you for your honesty. In my own experience, I've found that when I hit a pocket of big resistance to something that is a practice or healing tool, then I know I'm touching something deep. Every time I've walked through my fear and stepped toward rather than away from it, big transformations have happened.

It's similar to the process of getting defensive. Anytime someone criticizes me or accuses me of something and I get upset and defensive, that's a sign that I must agree with the criticism or accusation at some level, or that I am afraid it might be true. I have learned to watch for these reactions in myself, because they show me where I still need to grow.

Be gentle with yourself here, but also brave. Warrior Goddess Training can't hurt you. The worst thing that could happen is you read the book and do the exercises and learn very little. The upside is that you could discover new and wonderful things about your unique and precious self. My money is on the latter.

I support you in not forcing yourself, but rather *inviting* yourself to go forward. Stay with the intensity, and breathe through it. Notice what thoughts are arising. Lastly, let go of any expectations you have of what the "final you" is going to look like.

||||||||||||||||||||||||||||||||||||

Question

How do I quiet or push aside the voices of self-doubt and self-rejection—the ones even when I say, "Hello, you're beautiful"? There is a snake sliding around me saying, "Don't believe that. You're not worth the dirt you stand on." I'm a fighter and I push a lot, but I battle self-doubt a lot too.

Answer

Those voices of the judge and victim are so insidious. One thing that is helpful is to keep reminding yourself that these voices are not telling you the truth.

I recognize from your question that you are a "fighter" and that you "battle" self-doubt, but this is one area where I am going to ask you to do the opposite. Don't fight the judge or victim voice or even try to stop them for now—just learn to recognize them when they speak, and then say, "Thank you for sharing. I'm not interested." Then go back to talking kindly and compassionately to yourself. Oftentimes it's the fight within that the judge and victim feed on, and the one tactic they can't handle is to be lovingly acknowledged and then ignored. When you do this, they can behave like a small child having a tantrum, effectively saying, "Give me what I want! Pay attention to me!"

It will take awhile before these old voices get quieter, but I promise you they will. The less energy you feed them, the more they will dissipate. As Warrior Goddesses, our battle is to keep bringing our attention back to how we want to be in relationship with ourselves, and to not judge or fight the self-doubt, but rather to acknowledge it and know it is not us. Remember, these voices come from years of training many generations back, and they won't go away overnight.

You are beautiful. Giggle at the old voices—don't give them your power.

||||||||||||||||||||||||||||||||||||||||

Question

The book says that we need to have the "willingness to give up who we think we should be in favor of who we are," but I'm confused by what you mean here. Could you explain further?

Answer

I agree, that statement makes little logical sense at first view! But it is a profound truth that opens the door to immense healing and transformation.

When we stop fighting who we are and we stop trying to become someone else, we come into the present moment. This acceptance of what is right now creates space to love and accept ourselves for who we are right now. This doesn't mean we don't want to grow and stretch and transform; it means we are honest with where we are now and are willing to see the truth of this moment of our development.

Here is another way to think of it. If you are traveling and you are lost, the first thing you would do is stop and confirm where you are, and then find the path to where you want to go. If you keep saying, "But I shouldn't be here! I don't like this! I am doing it wrong!" and only look at where you wish you were, you'd stay lost.

Hating, shaming, beating yourself up for not being who you want to be, and using negative self-talk as a motivational force for change rarely, if ever, works, and it certainly doesn't yield permanent, positive change. Not to mention it isn't a very enjoyable process, either, to say the least. Until you accept and love who you are at this moment, you will stay trapped in a spiral of self-judgment and struggle.

This brings us to the Warrior Goddess path. Until you accept and love who you are at this moment, you will stay trapped in a spiral of self-judgment and struggle. Try acknowledging your struggle, and say to yourself, "Okay, this is where I am right now, and I choose to love and accept myself for who I am at this very moment." With this self-love and self-acceptance, you can then see any areas of your life that you would like to change, as these represent "where you want to go." Now you have a map based on self-love, and you can explore the most creative and enjoyable path to take you there.

Another magical thing that happens when you "give up who you think you should be in favor of who you are" is that in many areas, you find that who you are now is who you really wanted to be all along. In other words, when you look deeply into your heart and discover what *you* really want, and not what society, your inner judge, or your inner victim says you should want, you often find that what you want is what you already have.

|||||||||||||||||||||||||||||||||||||||||

Question

I find I occasionally have non-acceptance of others' thoughts or actions. I usually recognize this *after* I have said something or realized I thought/felt a judgment. This often happens when it involves those very close to me. How can I be more accepting of those I'm closest to?

Answer

It is wonderful that you have the awareness to recognize when you are having judging thoughts and feelings toward others, even if it is after-the-fact. It is this awareness that will help you change that behavior.

Also, it has been my experience that those we are closest to are also our greatest spiritual teachers. You don't need to go to an ashram, a monastery, or a mountaintop; the people you are living with are in the best position to show you where you still have room to grow.

To unwind the habit of judgment takes practice and perseverance. My first suggestion would be to bring your attention to where you judge yourself for the same type of behavior that you see in others. So often it's the things we don't like in other people that are also the things we don't like in ourselves. Other people are our mirrors, and what we are judging in them are just reflections of the ways we judge ourselves. So the first step is to find out what their actions can teach you about you.

Next, I invite you to explore what it means to really let people make their own choices and be who they are. By definition, if I'm judging someone it is because I think they should be different. In this way, I am not respecting their right to choose their own path. When you notice yourself being judgmental, ask yourself if it's possible to accept who and where they are at this time in their life. This doesn't mean you necessarily have to agree with the other person's behavior. You may choose to share with them how you feel, but if you do, be sure your words are coming from a place of love rather than fear or judgment, otherwise you will likely not help the situation. And remember, you can always set a boundary with this person or behavior.

Bringing forward your compassion and presence with those closest to you (and everyone else) will create a conscious response to a situation rather than an unconscious reaction or judgment. As you get better at recognizing where your judgments come from and realizing that others have a right to choose their own path, you'll also find that you notice your judgment sooner, *before* you say something. This is wonderful, because that's one less mess that needs a cleanup.

||||||||||||||||||||||||||||||||||||||

Question

The lesson on letting your heart be open sounds dangerous to me. I don't want to be guarded, but I don't want to be taken advantage of, either. How do I balance these two opposing ideas?

Answer

I love what you wrote. For me, it is the combination of innocence and wisdom, or vulnerability and clarity, which allows us to hold ourselves in deep love and share this with others, while also staying present with our boundaries and what works for us.

Much of the confusion comes when we equate opening our heart to *always* saying yes. Let me be clear on this: You can open your heart and say no simultaneously. As Warrior Goddesses, we want to keep an open heart in all situations, yet we insist on maintaining our own energy, safety, and needs. Doing both is the art of Warrior Goddess living, and it takes practice! The ten lessons and the accompanying exercises are designed to teach you how to do exactly this.

In the meantime, I would suggest that if you find yourself in a situation where you feel afraid to open your heart, you might ask yourself the following question: How can I open my heart and protect my energy, my safety, and my own needs? Go inside and listen for the answer.

Here's an example. I'd been on a few dates with someone I really liked, and the guy told me he was falling for me and wanted to spend the night. Although I liked him too, I wasn't ready to take our relationship to that level. I went inside and asked myself, How can I open my heart and protect my energy, my safety, and my own needs? I listened for direction. Then I said to him, "Sweetie, I am so glad you feel this way about me, and I really like you too, but I'm not comfortable with that step in our relationship until we know each other better."

He now had a choice: He could choose to support my feelings and continue to get to know me, without any guarantee of what that will bring, or he could choose to end the relationship. No matter which choice he made, I had opened my heart but protected my energy, safety, and needs, so I would be in a good place either way.

The thing to remember is that it's entirely possible to open your heart and say no simultaneously, and many times this is exactly what a Warrior Goddess needs to do.

|||||||||||||||||||||||||||||||||||||||||

Your Questions Answered

Question

I'm confused about acceptance. I am creative, funny, and eccentric; however, my loved ones criticize me for being different. What I call self-expression and free thinking they call desperate for attention and rebellious. Although I celebrate our differences, I'm ridiculed in return. What do you do when you feel like those around you aren't accepting you?

Answer

I love that you celebrate differences and are a free spirit! And sometimes those closest to us don't understand or want us to be more like them. I support you in finding other beings who accept you as you are and nourish your spirit, and in the meantime work on letting go of trying to get your loved ones to accept or like you; instead, practice simply accepting them and liking them just as they are. Remember, you can only control your own acceptance, not whether or not anyone else accepts you.

One thing I like to do when I get criticism is sift through it and see if there is anything that might be applicable to me, because even if 99 percent of it is projection, I want to find the 1 percent that is the gift that will help me to grow as a person.

It may take some time to find a local community that says yes to you, but if you stay focused on this and get creative in your search, I know you'll discover a place where you are supported and fit in. And you definitely fit in here with our Warrior Goddess tribe! May all who read this send you blessings and encouragement to continue to be your wonderful, creative self.

|||||||||||||||||||||||||||||||||||||

Question

I have been putting others' needs ahead of my own for so long that I really have no idea what I want for myself. I just feel completely lost. Do you have any suggestions?

Answer

Thank you for this question. So many women out there can relate to feeling this way.

My suggestion is to be gentle with yourself and start by finding out what you want in regards to the little things. For example, let's take a choice such as what you want for dinner, or what you want to watch on TV tonight. I invite you to really slow down before you make the decision and ask yourself: What do I really want? Does this serve me? How will this nourish me? Be willing to take chances as well as be creative with your choices. And if you choose something and then decide you don't like it, give yourself permission to take another action, to choose another path.

I know these tiny things might not seem all that important, but by honoring your choices with these little decisions you are creating a pattern of finding out and choosing what you want. Once your body recognizes what it feels like to honor your choices for the little things, some of the larger questions will be easier to answer. In this way, you will begin to equate an inner feeling of "yes" with an outer choice, and you will recognize that feeling when presented with significant choices.

Another great way to get in touch with what you really want is to imagine that inside of you there is an inner fire, and you want to help that fire burn brightly. What desires can you throw into the fire to make it blaze? What causes your fire to diminish? Be compassionate with yourself as you take responsibility for your choices, remembering that it's okay to choose again. It will take time, but you can learn how to support yourself and create the life you really want.

Question

There is someone in my life who continually tries to manipulate me. How can I stop them in a loving manner?

Answer

Thanks for writing. You can't stop people from trying to manipulate you or change your mind, but you can get steadier at listening to your own voice and setting clear, loving boundaries. What works for me is to remember that others have their own opinions, beliefs, and desires, and while I can listen to those, if something they are saying is making me more confused or is not feeling true to me, then I can acknowledge their position but also follow my own inner guidance. This is wisdom in action. When you find yourself in this situation, you may say something as simple as, "I hear that you want me to do X, but it feels best for me to do Y." In this way, you are using clear language that acknowledges the other person's point of view while stating what your needs are.

It takes practice to do this, especially if we have a history of trying not to disappoint or hurt others. Learning to share your needs while staying present with others' disappointment or desire for things to be different is a beautiful thing! Stay with it. And if someone is really not listening to you at all, even when you are clear, you might want to set some additional boundaries in the relationship or let that person know you are not interested in his or her opinion about certain things. Remember, you have the power of choosing your own actions, regardless of what someone else wants from you.

Question

After reading your book, I realized that ever since I was a teenager I placed all my value and self-worth on how attractive I looked on the outside, and I constantly sought acceptance from men to tell me how pretty I looked. I don't want that anymore. I want to find value in myself, but I feel like I have wasted so much time. Any suggestions?

Answer

First, forgive yourself for basing your sense of value on your external beauty only. As women, many of us were trained that our worth and value is relative to how beautiful we are to others. If others see us as beautiful, then we are okay; and if they don't, then we self-reject. Even if we meet others' standards and find self-acceptance in our beauty, this only sets up the fear that we are not going to be seen as beautiful or valuable in the future.

The truth is that you are only as beautiful and valuable as you feel you are, deep down. Value is not based on your looks, your weight, or having the latest fashion; it is based on how you feel about yourself and the light you shine.

Bring your focus to what you want to feel about yourself. Let go of the judgment and doubt that you've taken on, and keep redefining what makes you happy, what inspires you, and what you are passionate about. Toss out all the mirrors, and feel who you are from the inside out. The ego is always going to use external things to feel better or the image of who it thinks we should be against us. Go beneath the ego's voice to find your true, authentic knowing. Keep listening. The truth of the beauty of who you are is there, and it is an experience of celebrating life fully.

Finally, remember that it took every moment and every experience of your precious life to bring you to where you are now. Nothing was wasted, and not a thing is out of place.

||||||||||||||||||||||||||||||||||||

Question

I have been with my wife for over ten years. I am making magnificent changes within myself, but they are uncomfortable for her. How do I address her discomfort with these changes?

Answer

When we start to change and act in new ways, it is sometimes uncomfortable for those closest to us, who are familiar with who we were. One of the best things you can do is have a good heart-to-heart with her, letting her know that you care about your relationship with her and want to nourish it, and that you are also nourishing your relationship with yourself and changing some old patterns and habits that no longer serve you. Let her know how you think she will benefit from you making the changes you are seeking. Ask her if she has any fears, and share what your fears are, too. When we are willing to be vulnerable, we can open the door for more intimacy and communication.

Your wife may or may not be able to talk about her fears openly with you, but at least you will have started a dialogue and acknowledged that it might be uncomfortable. The next step is for you to get comfortable with her being uncomfortable! By acknowledging her discomfort without trying to fix, change, minimize, or apologize for it, you have opened the door to her finding a new level of comfort. And you will also learn how to stay steady and loving with yourself even when you are uncomfortable!

I congratulate you and celebrate all the changes you are making!

|||||||||||||||||||||||||||||||||||||||||

Question

I share joint custody of my son with my ex, and while our interactions around our son's welfare are not necessarily argumentative, they are not what I would call pleasant, either. I dread these encounters because they are uncomfortable. In general, how does a Warrior Goddess remain calm and relaxed in uncomfortable situations such as this?

Answer

Many of us have learned to move away from uncomfortable situations, to see them as something to avoid or even fear. When we start to see everything as a part of life, neither good nor bad, and stop trying to always be comfortable, we can learn to find the comfort in the uncomfortable.

When I am in situations where I feel uncomfortable, I've found it really helpful to start by breathing deeply into my belly. Doing this allows me to find my center, the place where I feel calm and still regardless of what is happening around me. This takes practice, but the ultimate benefit is that I am much more focused and relaxed in situations that previously were very stressful.

Start this breathing and centering practice with the small discomforts of your life, the places where you might get a little irritated or feel a bit uneasy. I call these grocery-store practices, because one of the best places to practice the little things is when you are out in the world with people you don't know.

When you notice that you feel a bit uncomfortable, say when someone steps in line in front of you or you notice a homeless person who makes you want to look away, take a breath. Explore the physical sensations of discomfort in your body. Take a breath. Invite your body to relax. You can breathe into your shoulders, loosen your jaw, wiggle your toes. Let your body know you are okay. As you relax, find your sense of inner calm. You might still feel uncomfortable, but now you will be present with the discomfort. Simply be with it, rather than trying to avoid it or fix it. As you practice your grocery-store moments you'll gain strength, and then you can start to bring your awareness to finding relaxation and calm in more difficult encounters, like the ones with your son's father.

||||||||||||||||||||||||||||||||||

Question

My intimate relationships all look the same: I give and give and give, always putting others ahead of me. But no matter what I do, they all ultimately leave. My father abandoned me when I was young, and I feel like the men I pick are all incarnations of him. I want

a real relationship with someone, an equal partnership, but I continually fail in this area. Is there anything else I can do?

Answer

Dear one. It's so hard to see our own inherent beauty when we
abandon ourselves to pursue love or attention from others. One
of the first things to do is forgive yourself and bring in your compassion for the little-girl part of you who has tried so hard to get
love and be safe. That little girl inside needs you! And when you
listen to the voice of your internal judge and blame yourself, you
unintentionally abandon her and yourself.

Before you can really be in a relationship with someone else,
you first have to attend to your most important relationship: the
one with yourself. Then, when you feel that you are seeing and
being with yourself in a new way, you can evaluate what you want
from a relationship with another. At this point, you will no longer be coming from a place of fear and scarcity, because you will
know that you are the most important relationship of your life.

|||||||||||||||||||||||||||||||||||||||

Question

What can I do to have a better acceptance of my
body? I get very self-conscious about my body when
I'm around men, and I can't seem to make that feeling
go away. I am considering plastic surgery to boost my
confidence.

Answer

Oh dear one, you are so beautiful and perfect exactly the way you are!

Body image is a topic many of us have dealt with at one point or another, so let's review the origin of these issues. As humans, we are not born with any concept of what our body "should" or "should not" look like; we add these ideas based on society's preferences as we grow up. Not surprisingly, different cultures at different times throughout history have decided that varying degrees of size, shape, shade, and age were somehow "better" than others. When you take a step back, you can see how arbitrary these likes and dislikes can be, and it becomes much easier to love the body you have rather than wish for the one you don't.

While it can take generations for societal preferences to change, you can change your relationship with yourself and your body starting right now. But this isn't an easy task—it's going to take your willingness, patience, and Warrior Goddess perseverance to shift to accepting yourself exactly as you are. There is no pill you can take to suddenly like your lips or your hips, but here are some actions steps that will move you in that direction.

First, every time you look in the mirror, say something nice about yourself. Yes, it may feel fake, awkward, or silly at first, but keep doing it. Remember, you are undoing a very long pattern, and it's going to take time. You may say something like, "You are so beautiful," or "I love your hair." Start by saying something nice about the areas that feel most genuine, and then look at the places you would rather change, noticing their uniqueness as well.

Second, try to stop comparing yourself to magazines, friends, coworkers, or anyone else who has a body that is closer to the image of perfection you have been carrying around with you for years. The very act of noticing when you do this is the beginning of the end of these comparisons. When you hear the thoughts of comparison in your mind, say to yourself, "Thank you, but I love the body I have. It's perfect for me."

Third, take a moment to look at the real women in your life, not the ones who have been touched up in magazines and on TV. Look at their lips, hips, and other body parts. Notice how we are all "flawed" in some way based on society's preferences, which really means we are all perfect, exactly the way we are!

Lastly, I would suggest you wait on the plastic surgery until you've done all the lessons in this book. I have nothing against such procedures, but I want you to be sure that you are undertaking any such procedure to empower yourself rather than please someone else.

Remember, as a Warrior Goddess woman you don't have to look or be any particular way. The point of Warrior Goddess Training is to find out who you really are and what you really want, and then making a conscious decision to live in your own authenticity.

IIIIIIIIIIIIIIIIIIIIIIIIIIIIIIIIIIIIIIII

Question

At one point in your teaching I panicked when I realized you were asking me to be a cheerleader and supporter of *myself*. Before that moment, I thought you were preparing me to be supportive of other women taking the course. I'm a fantastic supporter of others, but how do I shift to become an avid supporter of myself?

Answer

If you are a fantastic supporter of others, then you have all the ingredients necessary to support YOU! It just takes bringing all that yummy energy you share with others to yourself. Here's a tip: When you notice that you are judging yourself, stop and ask what you would say to your best friend in the same situation. Bring that voice to yourself. At first it might feel awkward or a bit forced, but over time you will trade in that old judgmental talk for the lightness of loving, you-can-do-it words. Sometimes, literally talking to yourself out loud helps to bring that supportive part of you forward. You have a habit of not supporting yourself; now make a new habit of listening for what you need and giving it to yourself!

||||||||||||||||||||||||||||||||||||||

Question

I get that nothing can harm the real you, but I am terrified of pain—the intense, prolonged sort of pain that comes from radical surgery that absolutely drains you for months or years—and trauma. I've experience both over the past four years, and I'm pretty frozen wanting to shield myself from any more pain. How do you find the grace to make it through events that shatter you without going into a hole and never coming out?

Answer

I am sorry that you have had to deal with so much pain and trauma recently. When we have trauma and pain as an ongoing experience, it can get locked in our body and make us go into a sort of paralysis to protect ourselves. I love that you are wanting to find grace and peace within.

You can start to unwind the fear and thaw the rigid places by first being compassionate with your body. Praise your body, nourish it, and listen to what it needs. Thank it for the gifts it brings to you. You might have to keep moving through the pain and fear to find what feels good in your being: perhaps your ankles feel strong, or your face feels relaxed. Start small, naming what you feel gratitude for, the pain-free places. Also celebrate your stamina, your resilience, and your courage. Be with what is without judging it, linking it to the past, or worrying about the future.

This is easier said than done, but it is a practice, along with gratitude and celebrating the little things, that will lead you to inner grace. Let your body know it is okay that it is afraid, and that you will stay with yourself. Breathe into the fear. Be gentle with yourself, but fierce in your self-love. Lastly, know that you are being supported from afar by me and other Warrior Goddess sisters as you travel this heroine's journey.

|||||||||||||||||||||||||||||||||||||||

ABOUT THE AUTHOR

© Nicholas Rozsa

HeatherAsh Amara is the author of *Warrior Goddess Training: Become the Woman You Are Meant to Be* and *The Toltec Path of Transformation: Embracing the Four Elements of Change.*

She is dedicated to supporting women and men in becoming more curious, open, courageous, humorous, creative, loving, accepting and impeccable explorers of their truth.

www.heatherashamara.com

Notes

Notes

Notes

Notes

Notes